Natural Building Techniques

Natural Building Techniques

A GUIDE TO ECOLOGICAL METHODS AND MATERIALS

Tom Woolley

THE CROWOOD PRESS

First published in 2022 by
The Crowood Press Ltd
Ramsbury, Marlborough
Wiltshire SN8 2HR

enquiries@crowood.com
www.crowood.com

British Library Cataloguing-in-Publication Data
A catalogue record for this book is available from the British Library.

ISBN 978 0 7198 4047 0

Cover design: Maggie Mellett
Front cover: earth wall in house in Fifeshire, Scotland (photo: Becky Little); back cover top: interior CLT finished walls, Adderstone Crescent (photo: Eurban); back cover bottom: cob handrail by Becky Little (photo: Becky Little)

Disclaimer
Every effort has been made by the authors and the publishers to check the accuracy of information contained in this book however readers are encouraged to use this information as a starting point only. It will be necessary to check for updated contact and product information as this will change over time. It is also important to obtain the best possible professional advice about design, construction and material specification when undertaking a project. The author cannot take responsibility for any building or design work decisions based on ideas found in this book.

Dedication
In memory of Heimir Salt,
natural-born anarchist and self-builder

Typeset by Simon and Sons
Printed and bound in India by Replika Press Pvt. Ltd.

Contents

I AM ALWAYS AMAZED AT THE AMOUNT OF material and sheer hard work it takes to erect a building. Even a small house takes truckloads of the stuff, with fittings and materials coming from just about everywhere on the face of the planet. Sadly, the end result is architecture that is often badly built, barely fit for human habitation, and toxic to life. We are destroying our relationship with the natural world as we huddle behind triple-glazed windows in mechanically ventilated rooms, disconnected from experience of nearly everything outside. Human activities are so huge now that by the end of 2020 human-made materials outweighed Earth's entire biomass. Around 1900 this figure ran at about 3 per cent. The twentieth century certainly was a very busy one!

Human activity has brought about a new geological era, the Anthropocene. Or as some would have it, the 'Plasticene', now that plastic and synthetic particles are found in every corner of the globe, where they will become trapped in the geological record for all time. No part of Planet Earth has escaped the influence of humans upon it. Everyone by now must be aware of the cluster of major and dire environmental issues facing us all, brought about by this impact.

The major action that drives all this frantic activity is the built environment, wrecking the natural environment in its wake. It is the natural environment that sustains us, nourishes us, gives us life and provides essential life support. Everything we use to build with is won from the earth, cut down, dug up, transported, processed, often made toxic, and usually with huge energy inputs and environmental damage.

Architecture (a term that includes the whole built environment) that does not sustain and enhance the natural environment is killing us and every other living organism. We are now in the midst of the sixth mass extinction period, brought about by human destruction.

We have been forewarned by scientists about the consequences of burning fossil fuels since the end of the nineteenth century. Rachel Carson's pivotal *Silent Spring* in the 1950s warned us about persistent toxins in our environment. We are slow learners.

Given what we have collectively wrought, collectively we need to change our attitude to our built environment if things are ever to improve. What we build now, what we build with, how we build, where we build, the layout of cities, how we move about, and how we refurbish, have consequences that will last for centuries.

We know it is critical that we immediately reduce embodied energy by very large amounts and eliminate toxins from our buildings. Emissions released now are the ones that need urgent attention if we are to decarbonize rapidly enough to avoid even worse climate-related disasters than those already occurring all around the world.

Therefore, the most ecological building is the one you don't build. If you can't do it well, do nothing. Next it is the one you don't demolish. We simply can't afford to trash the embodied energy already expended. And then, if we must build, it's the one that treads carefully, using local minimally processed resources, erecting buildings that meet real need and not pandering to greed.

Death by a thousand cuts destroys and poisons the natural environment. We need to kill the notion that any action we take can be regarded as no more than minor, with its underlying assumption that the environment can sustain an ongoing and ever-increasing assault on its health by an ever-increasing expansion of the built environment, even if it's only one small incursion at a time. The critical question above all other considerations has to become whether any proposal or action enhances or degrades the natural environment. It's a simple test.

This earth-centric approach is critical as the foundation of any built environment that will protect and restore the wider encompassing environment.

There is urgency in addressing the issues facing us. To do this we have to work with what we know now. The materials we choose to work with matter. One of the progressive and forward-looking keys to creating a better built environment uses what are collectively referred to as natural materials. These are locally found, won and modified with minimal processing, are non-toxic in nature, and often have been worked with and used over thousands of years.

Humans have built since antiquity with natural timbers and have used natural fibres in many ways. Earth-building techniques, often with the addition of natural fibres such as straw, have a history running back at least 10,000 years, so are arguably good for a few more years yet. Burning lime for mortar and whitewash tracks back at least 2,000 years. Mixing lime with hemp has nearly as long a history. More recently we have the addition of strawbale building to add to our mix of materials and techniques. They all have low embodied energy or even sequester carbon, and they do not rely on widespread use of poisons.

We are very fortunate to have people amongst us who know how to build really well using a wide range of natural materials, building on that very long tradition of their local and international use. In more recent times, these techniques have been subjected to a lot of research to demonstrate their strength and durability, and readily pass modern building performance criteria. Not only can they create well-performing buildings, but they use techniques often readily adopted by owner-builders as well as professional builders. They create buildings that are readily appreciated for their beauty but that also have an intangible, almost visceral, appeal.

This new book by Tom Woolley is a wide-ranging overview of the state of knowledge about many such building materials and techniques, drawn from his passion, experience and long career advocating for their use.

I am based on the other side of the globe but have no hesitation in hoping for the wide distribution and uptake of the accumulated wisdom and knowledge that my colleague has worked so hard to present in this book. It is mainly focused on the UK, but it has much wider application as well. As to the planet and all who live on it – we all depend on it.

Graeme North, MNZM FNZIA
Founding Chair of the Earth Building
Association of New Zealand
Chair of the Standards New Zealand Technical
Committee for NZ Earth Building Standards
Member of the New Zealand Order of Merit
August 2021

HUNDREDS OF PEOPLE HAVE CONTRIBUTED to the production of this book by enthusiastically sending details of projects and photos and by discussing ideas with me; some of these knew me but others were new lockdown friends whom I am yet to meet. It wasn't possible to list them all here but I am grateful to them all. All other images are by the author unless specified otherwise. I need to thank The Crowood Press and Graeme in New Zealand for their critical support. At home I need to thank Rachel, Hannah, Jack and Lisa for putting up with me, and Sophie, Cathy, Olly and Chantelle for being there.

A special acknowledgement goes to Heimir Salt, whom I first met when teaching at the Architectural Association in London. He was central to the development of the innovative alternative approach to architecture that grew out of five years' intense work with community and housing groups influenced by Colin Ward and Walter Segal. He also took a leading role in the research and publication of an important report on self-build in Britain, and later set up a useful website, 'Self-Build Central', which featured many case studies and information which must have helped hundreds of natural and self-builders throughout the UK. Heimir was one of the first people I knew who lived a non-consumerist lifestyle, always able to live happily on very little and able to find whatever was needed to do low-impact building. As a modest and unassuming person his life will not be well recorded elsewhere, which is why it was important to mention him in this book, which probably wouldn't have happened without his influence.

Chapter One

THE IMPORTANCE OF NATURAL BUILDING

Why is Natural Building Important?

In a rapidly changing world, many of the things that we now take for granted may no longer be possible. Finding affordable building materials is becoming a problem. The UK has a major housing shortage, but development of low-cost affordable homes is still very limited and even renting a house seems out of sight for many young people. Shortage of land and sites remains a problem and cost of construction materials is escalating. Despite a great deal of talk about zero-carbon targets, little is changing in terms of how conventional buildings are built and energy costs are increasing in heating homes which are poorly insulated, including many new homes that are meant to be more energy-efficient.

Building and renovating with natural materials provides a real opportunity for people who want to live in a healthy ecological home, while making a significant contribution to reducing CO_2 emissions. This book gives an outline of many of the materials, products and methods of construction that are available. For some, building a cob oven or a strawbale cabin in the back garden is a hobby activity and for others it involves searching for a new ecological lifestyle, but natural building goes further than this; it creates a whole new approach to construction that has a lower impact than conventional mainstream development. For many, using low-impact materials may become the only way to create an affordable solution.

Natural materials are widely available from a wide range of sources, including what are known as bio-based materials such as straw and hemp, which can be grown on farms in the UK and Ireland. Earth and clay can be dug up from the building site if you are lucky. Wood-based products are largely imported

Hempcrete Cottage, Co. Down. (Photo: Rachel Bevan)

from other parts of the world but could be made closer to home. Other key materials like lime are largely imported but much more could be done to use sources in the UK and Ireland.

Unfortunately, there remains an anxiety that natural materials are not robust enough to withstand the weather and that they will rot and decay. Architects prefer to import endangered species such as cedar or use wood treated with chemicals rather than local timber. We have become so dependent on cement and concrete and a wide range of plastics that are preferred when buildings are designed or renovated. Cement, concrete and plastic materials and gas-guzzling buildings (heating and air conditioning) are responsible for 40 per cent of global CO_2 emissions, and yet little thought is given to changing

Plastic-free housing, Redditch, by Accord Housing Association, currently under construction. (Photo: Accord)

but the use of plastic and synthetic materials has increased dramatically in the past twenty to thirty years and this is discussed in more detail in the final chapter. It is feasible to avoid and limit the use of plastics and synthetics by using natural materials and this has to be attractive to those of us who work hard to recycle household waste and avoid the use of single-use plastics. Campaigners like David Attenborough have done a wonderful job to make us aware of the terrible problems of plastic pollution, but this is seen as an issue of consumer waste, whereas plastic waste from buildings is one of the biggest sources of pollution. More details about conventional plastic and concrete housing are discussed in the final chapter, but Accord Housing Association, in the English Midlands, is building an innovative housing development in Redditch that is claimed to be plastic-free. It's not 100 per cent plastic-free but they have gone a long way towards this target and also used natural materials such as wood fibre boards. (1)

to natural low-impact alternatives. Specifiers and quantity surveyors will artificially inflate prices for natural materials because they say that builders are unfamiliar with them, or they are difficult to source. This book will try to challenge these misconceptions.

Research for this book uncovered many examples of people who had been talked out of using natural materials by their architects or builders. Others used some natural materials but then added flammable plastic foam insulations as they were told that insulation standards would not be met. One aim of this book is to give you confidence that when you hope to build or renovate a home that natural materials are the best option and can be used successfully. There are many other obstacles and problems to be overcome, including shocking opposition from green campaigners, but in order to avoid a depressing start these issues are left to the final chapter, which you can ignore unless you want to know more about how to deal with these problems! Despite this, there are many, many people who have forged ahead building a huge range of natural buildings with great success, a sample of which are illustrated here.

Plastic-Free Building

Increasingly, our buildings are made of plastic. This may not be at all obvious when looking at a building apparently made of brick, concrete, timber and glass,

What are the Advantages of Natural Materials?

Natural materials, if used correctly, can make it possible to significantly limit the use of plastics, but it is important to go through with this rather than making compromises. Houses built with hempcrete or straw bales and even earth have been wrapped in plastic airtightness membranes with plastic foam insulation added because an energy 'expert' has said that it is necessary to comply with building regulations, but it's not necessary to be tricked into this! Natural materials can create buildings which are 'breathable', which is far better for your health and the health of the building. Wrapping buildings in plastic to make them more airtight was introduced to make buildings more energy-efficient but can lead to serious problems with damp, mould and health.

Breathability, or to use the correct term 'vapour permeability', allows buildings to cope with moisture and many natural materials are also hygroscopic, so they can help to regulate humidity and dampness. Many synthetic and conventional materials used today have the opposite effect, leading to 'sick' buildings, but natural materials provide the antidote to this.

Despite misinformation, many natural materials are fire-resistant without the use of toxic flame retardants. The average conventional house uses a huge chemical dose of hazardous chemical flame retardants, which are added to insulations, finishes, furniture and fittings. These chemicals are endocrine-disrupting chemicals which, even in small concentrations, can be absorbed through the endocrine system in the body and passed through the placenta to unborn babies as well as reducing testosterone in men. We inhabit a world of chemical soup in food, traffic pollution and, worst of all, in our buildings, producing a whole host of health problems such as developmental and behavioural issues in children and a significant increase in cancer levels. Some members of the medical and scientific community in the UK have their heads in the sand about environmental causes of cancer and other modern health problems, preferring to blame inherited conditions, lifestyle and obesity while ignoring the problem of hazardous emissions from buildings. Changing to natural materials is an escape from chemical pollution and giving a better start in life to your children. These issues are examined in much greater depth in another book (2) and a further volume should be out later in 2022.

An Architectural Theory of Natural Materials?

An excellent book entitled *Vegetarian Architecture* by Andrea Bocco Guaneri sets out the architectural and philosophical principles of natural building. This beautifully illustrated book includes many case studies of modern architecture that have drawn inspiration from the use of natural materials and vernacular traditions, and is worth a read to inspire you and maybe convert your sceptical architect. (3)

Many people have moved towards a more vegetarian diet for both health and environmental reasons. Building with conventional materials might now be compared to living on a diet of steaks, burgers and chicken nuggets, so the vegetarian metaphor is relevant. Guaneri quotes Lewis Mumford, who coined the term 'biotechnic' as an ecologically compatible approach to technology. He argues that as we become increasingly dependent on technology there is an alternative approach of 'doing simple things with simple means'. Mumford compared machine technology to 'organic technology', the latter based on building by 'craftsmen of necessity', meeting everyday needs with limited local resources. Guaneri goes on to quote Ernst Schumacher who saw the technology of mass production as inherently violent, ecologically damaging, and self-defeating in terms of non-renewable resources. Building according to the laws of ecology is gentle in its use of scarce resources, designed to serve the human person.

Natural building is about thrift and using materials and technologies that are kind to humans and the planet by valuing and making responsible use of scarce and renewable resources. Making these choices may be easier after reading this book

Beware Greenwash

However, just as multinational agri-businesses have jumped onto veganism as yet another consumerist route to profits, it is important to beware greenwash. The construction materials industry and many architects talk of green and eco buildings that continue to use mass-produced, synthetic, CO_2-emitting toxic materials. There are even 'vegan' and 'feng shui' paints that must be seen for what they are – cunning marketing. This book explores the world of manufactured natural materials and where they can be found. Many of us will have to make pragmatic choices and try to move towards natural materials, because digging up some clay and cutting down nearby trees is not always feasible. This book does not advocate competition between which is the greenest or most natural solution and whether strawbale is better than cob or hempcrete but it does encourage making principled practical and pragmatic choices. It also does not seek to condemn those who use natural materials combined with synthetic petrochemical products as at least they are moving in the right direction, but choosing earth, strawbale or hempcrete involves a rational evaluation of all the possibilities.

Some people like to build what inevitably get called 'hobbit houses', using a particular style of construction with rounded walls and reciprocal green roofs, maybe partially underground, and some of these may have the best and least impact of any of the projects featured in this book. However, the hobbit houses at Hobbiton in New Zealand, used in the *Hobbit* movies, were built out of polystyrene and plywood, later replaced by concrete and bricks, with a fake glass fibre tree, which seems a sad form of inspiration for natural builders. (4) Some eco enthusiasts use the term 'hobbit house' as synonymous with natural building, but natural low-impact houses can look exactly the same as conventional-build buildings and still be saving carbon and providing a healthier environment.

Why Use Natural Materials?

The aim of this book is to show how buildings can be constructed from natural materials, whether they are a plain bungalow or university offices, because unless we can change mainstream development to low-impact solutions, we cannot hope to achieve a zero-carbon society. Sadly, this is not yet understood by the hundreds of organizations calling for decarbonization, including many green campaigners who follow fake trails to decarbonization (which are discussed in the final chapter) as they fail to embrace the principles of natural building. Fortunately, there are many more people using natural materials than there were in 2006 and natural building can no longer be regarded as a marginal approach to construction. Natural materials can be used to create whatever style of house you want, from an approach that expresses the vernacular and natural features of materials to a minimal modernist approach.

Hempcrete house in the Isle of Man. (Photo: Nigel Kermode)

The other key aspect of this book is the provision of convincing evidence that natural materials actually work as well as if not better than conventional ones. To use natural materials can mean having a better-quality environment that is more energy-efficient and robust. Detractors push the idea that natural buildings are second best but modern lightweight synthetic plastic buildings lack thermal mass and the ability to regulate humidity and air quality. Cheap conversions of office buildings into flats, for instance, which is becoming commonplace to meet housing needs, puts occupants at even greater risk from poor conditions, particularly overheating in heatwaves, as builders use lightweight synthetic products if and when they bother to add insulation. (5)

Natural materials like hempcrete, straw, wood fibre and earth behave in a completely different way from conventional materials, allowing buildings to store energy in the fabric. These materials are also robust and long-lasting and able to deal with weather and climate. Timber preserved with lime, wattle and daub, and cob walls have survived for centuries and yet architects prefer to specify untried plastic materials that may last little more than twenty years. Embracing natural materials is about re-establishing contact with a vernacular tradition, but doing so in modern ways.

The Changing Context for Building

As this book was nearing completion, the media was full of reports about increasing fuel and electricity costs that have only been held back by government price caps. Those on limited incomes will find it harder to heat their homes and keep the lights on in the future as prices rise. Pressure to apply inappropriate approaches to decarbonization is leading to calls for gas boilers and woodburning stoves to be banned and regulations are likely to insist on electrical heating only in the future. This will create greater dependence on the giant electricity companies and, even though increasing amounts of electricity are coming from renewables, this is mostly in the hands of multinationals. It will be hard to hide from the zero-carbon 'police' when they spot smoke coming out of your chimney and we will be forced to adopt technologies like air-source heat pumps or pumping hydrogen down old gas pipes. This might sound like a luddite perspective but the energy campaigners spend little of their time on issues like embodied energy, better insulation and healthy buildings, hoping instead for some kind of 'techno-salvation'.

Natural building gives you an opportunity to keep yourself warm in a healthy way and a really well-designed vapour-permeable house with good thermal mass will make it possible to keep the heating bills down. This low-technology approach will last much longer than new gadgets.

The other issue which is currently attracting a massive amount of panic reporting is the cost and shortages of materials. This means that timber, imported timber and timber products are becoming much more expensive and even in short supply. A lime materials supplier in England has said that it is hard to get deliveries of raw materials as many trucks in the England have been diverted to supply concrete and aggregates to the HS2 high-speed railway line construction and there is also a shortage of HGV drivers. What could be better reasons for using locally sourced natural materials where possible and this will be even more essential in the future. Natural builders can potentially look after themselves, while also having much less impact on the planet.

The latest revelations about climate change accompanied by catastrophic flooding, heatwaves, forest fires and storms should be taken seriously but it's possible that many people have become numb to these issues. The Sixth IPCC Report presents data which cannot be challenged but does not tell us what we should do about it. (6) Seventy per cent of damaging emissions are caused by 100 of the main multinational companies but they continue with business as usual, blaming governments and ordinary people. They are even able to make use of procedures called 'corporate courts' which are built into international trade deals and are being used by corporations to block progressive environmental policies. (7)

These trade deals can affect the exploitation of resources and the transportation of toxic oil-based materials around the world. The manufacture of dangerous polluting materials such as isocyanates have effectively been stopped in Europe, but instead of changing to safe bio-based materials, production of plastic foam insulations has been moved to China and other Asian countries, leading to a spike in CFC (chlorofluorocarbon) emissions even though they were banned in the Montreal Protocol in 1992. Such materials are then shipped around the world to feed production of synthetic insulations in the UK and Ireland. (8)

We might feel guilty about our own personal behaviour but we need to challenge the big organizations that are really doing the damage. The multinational-owned building materials and construction industry wants us to continue to use toxic plastic petrochemical products and quarry for more and more non-renewable materials to make cement, concrete and mineral products. By building and renovating with natural materials it is possible to take a real stand against climate damage and show others the way forward. Natural buildings have to be a beacon of hope for a different way of respecting the planet and using resources responsibly. We need to lead by positive example rather than becoming depressed at all the stories of doom and gloom. You will search in vain in the IPCC and other reports on climate change for any guidance or practical proposals of what can be done, apart from expensive and possibly unrealistic high embodied-energy schemes such as storing CO_2 underground or converting gas pipes in the street to distribute hydrogen. Spreading woe about climate catastrophe is pointless if real alternatives are not on offer.

Self-Build is Good for the Soul

Using natural materials can have enormous psychological benefits. A house built and finished with wood and clay and natural paints not only has lower emissions but has a positive effect on mental health. Evidence for this is inevitably anecdotal, but work is beginning to promote the importance of the environment in terms of well-being. The UK Town and Country Planning Association has recognized this and introduced a private member's bill into the Westminster parliament promoting the concept of healthy housing. This holistic approach includes requirements for better external space as well as good indoor air quality. There are a handful of small private developers who are attempting to respond to this, but there seems to be little evidence of mainstream developers and social housing bodies recognizing the need and turning to greater use of natural materials. (9)

It is vitally important that natural building materials are affordable and not seen only as an expensive indulgence for wealthy people. Some housing developments marketed as healthy are trying to cash in on a demand from people who assume that such housing will be more expensive. There are one or two builders' merchants, selling imported materials, that tend to give the impression that they are catering for a luxury market. Some of the projects illustrated in this book may appear to fall into this category but, in most cases, reflect the efforts of people who have chosen natural solutions due to a restricted budget. Healthy materials could play a massive role in improving conditions for low-income people living with fuel poverty and health problems from cold and damp housing.

There are encouraging signs that new building companies and organizations providing training and advice are emerging. New businesses are being established to process hemp and provide bio-based insulation materials and possibly using local timber resources rather than relying on imports from Europe. Consumer demand can make a difference by persuading public bodies and private industry that renewable materials are the way forward and, if more widely available, can be used in low-cost building and renovation projects.

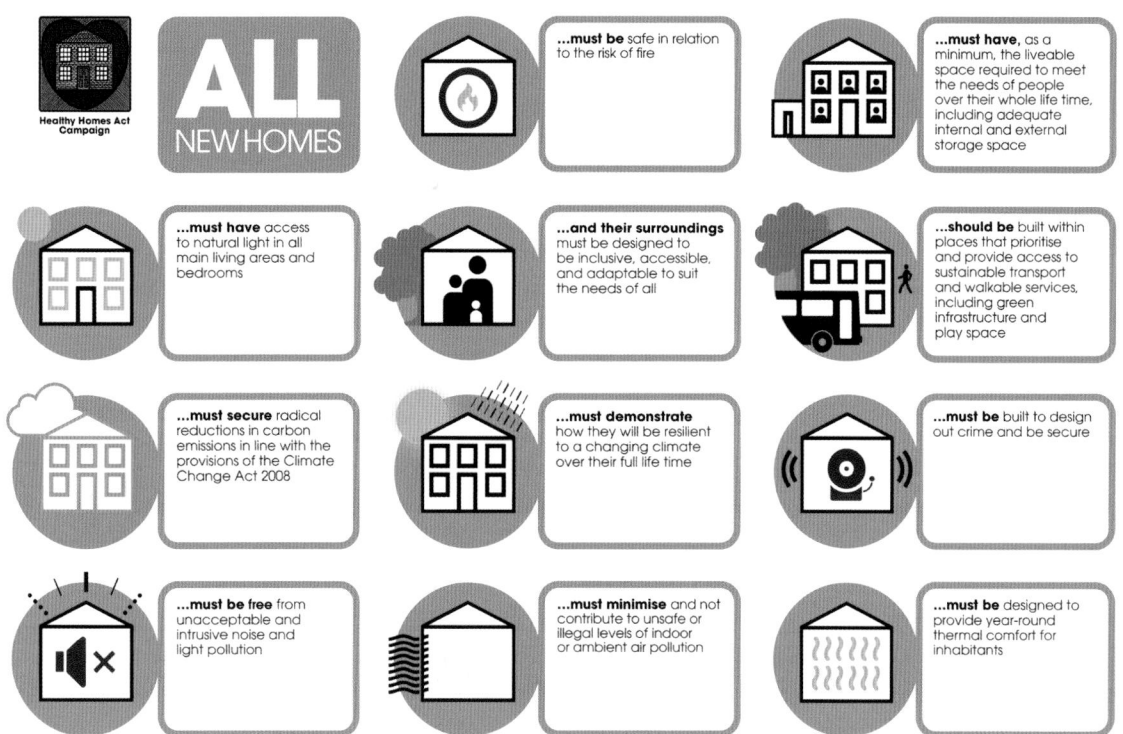

Town and Country Planning Association (TCPA) infographic about the Healthy Homes Bill. (Drawing: TCPA)

The Pent-Up Demand for Alternative Ways of Living

There has been a significant growth throughout the UK and Ireland of the number of individuals and groups wanting to live in a different way from conventional housing. Ben Fogle's TV programme *New Lives in the Wild* has provided examples of people who have given up city jobs and lifestyles to live off-grid and in a more ecological way. (10) Many of the people featured by Fogle have built houses that use natural and recycled materials and there are many, many more than have featured in TV programmes.

There has also been a huge growth in the development of so called glamping accommodation as demand for staycation holidays has grown. There are many commercial glamping-style holiday cabins, some of which are far from ecological or natural, using prefabricated building systems full of plastic foam insulation and recycled steel containers, but other projects use natural materials. There are cabins, pods, yurts and even tree houses to be found and it is estimated that the global glamping market is worth nearly £1.5 billion. (11) Glamping has been cynically described as for people who want to go camping but who still want an en suite toilet and don't want the hassle of putting up a tent! Do not assume that because the word 'glamping' is used that this means that buildings are healthy and environmentally friendly, but staying in a remote hut in the woods is inspiring many people to think that this could be a way to live in the future.

Scotland has led the way for people to experience life in the wilderness with the Thousand Huts programme, (12) established by the Reforesting Scotland campaign (13) and with a website full of useful information including how to build using low-impact and low-carbon methods. In Wales the One Planet Living planning policy (14) has established the possibility for planning permission to be given to people who want to live off-grid, sustainable, self-sufficient lives in the countryside. One Planet Living is highly regarded as a new policy although it is sometimes a struggle for those trying to establish this to get planning permission and meet the very stringent criteria.

A growing number of people are looking to alternative settlements, working co-operatively to establish eco villages or small eco developments. These can include self-build groups, co-housing groups and community land trusts, as well as eco villages. There are a range of organizations supporting or leading such initiatives, including the Ecological Land Co-operative, (15) Co-Housing UK (16) and Community Land Trust UK (17).

Finding land and finance are huge obstacles for people involved in these projects and even when they find a site, getting planning permission can be a struggle, with opposition from local people, parish councils and so on. The tremendous work of the Ecological Land Co-operative is worth studying, with details of their sites at Orchard Park (Cornwall),

Sparkford (Somerset), Furzehill (Gower), Arlington (East Sussex) and Greenham Reach (Devon). It is worth looking at the information on the Furzehill scheme in the Gower in South Wales. (18) Click on the link to the planning portal and download the massive range of documents that have been expertly put together to support the proposal, including many supporting letters and a few objections!

Many of these projects are not just about building eco houses but are also about growing vegetables and managing and rewilding land in a sustainable way. Sadly, few of the co-housing and community land trust projects have embraced natural building principles to date. To some extent this is understandable, as the effort required to establish these projects is so enormous that the groups are easily talked out of innovative construction approaches at the stage where they are exhausted. Many end up with mainstream architects, but even those determined to be green and energy-efficient have been persuaded to use synthetic petrochemical and concrete building solutions. There are exceptions, such as LILAC (Low Impact Living Affordable Community) in Leeds (*see* Chapter 5 on strawbale construction) and other projects which are long-established, such as Lammas in West Wales or Cloughjordan eco village in County

Part of Cloughjordan eco village, with a view of a hostel building near the entrance.

Cob roundhouse at Cloughjordan.

Hempcrete house at Cloughjordan.

Lammas Community Hub building.

One of many natural houses at Lammas, inevitably described by the press as a 'hobbit house'.

Use of local timber to create a platform bed in a house at Lammas.

Tipperary in Ireland. (19) These large projects contain many exemplary natural buildings using a wide range of techniques, including cob, straw, hempcrete and recycled materials, although establishing and maintaining big projects like this is not easy and can run into problems. (20) Eco villages can attract hordes of social science students, each keen to write a thesis about new ways of living. Lammas, however, have embraced this, and provide an excellent web resource with access to dozens of theses and their own annual monitoring reports. (21) (22) Eco villages are part of a global movement (23) (24) and many new projects can be found throughout the UK and Ireland.

Another vital source of information about a radical approach to the use of land, containing a great resource of stories and news about alternative projects, is *The Land* magazine – well worth subscribing to and excellent value for money. (25)

An Irish organization, IRLT (Irish Regenerative Land Trust), also sets out the basis for a new approach to the land, not just in Ireland but throughout Europe. (26) This began as part of a small project with some alternative land and housing groups in Ireland, funded by the Sustainable Housing for Inclusive and Cohesive Cities project (SHICC). (27) Following discussion with one of the land regeneration groups, a draft set of principles for sustainable housing development was prepared:

- Houses should be low-impact in terms of embodied energy and environmental impact, with responsible resource consumption based on a holistic approach.
- Re-use of existing buildings preferred to new-build, with regeneration and integration into local settlement patterns. (The principles below can largely apply to renovation and retrofit as well as newbuild.)
- Holistic design in terms of relationship with surrounding area and the potential for growing food, including sheltered outside area for clothes drying and good internal connection with outdoors and views of outside.
- Siting and orientation based on natural intuitive and indigenous understanding, touching the earth lightly, with minimal damage to existing site, beauty, harmony and enhancement of life and mental health. Sensitive positioning on site important.
- Nearly plastic-free, with minimal petrochemical material use and very low toxic emissions but with the use of fire-safe materials. Minimal use of cement, sand, concrete and polymers and plastics.
- Use of natural materials such as timber, earth, clay and lime with natural roofing such as slate and recycled plastic-free materials and components. Green roofs and green walls to avoid plastic materials if possible.
- Principled, careful, pragmatic use of less eco-friendly materials when unavoidable.
- Construction to be robust and long-lasting, with potential for dismantling, re-use and recycling of materials.

- High standard of thermal insulation with thermal mass and good thermal performance using breathable hygroscopic renewable bio-based materials and natural low-or zero-VOC (volatile organic compound) finishes.
- Recognition that extreme so-called zero-carbon aims cannot be achieved.
- Minimal use of toxic sealants, glues, preservatives and fungicides.
- Flexible, adaptable and accessible layout with space for storage and recycling.
- Natural ventilated pantry food storage to minimize use of electrical cooling.
- Passive solar gain but avoiding overheating with natural and cross-ventilation and good daylighting.
- Minimal use of mechanical ventilation.
- Use of natural and humanistic- (biophilic-) centred materials and interior design.
- Responsible collection and use of water, with use of urine separation and compost toilets where possible. Sewage waste to natural reedbed treatment if space available.
- Space heating and hot water kept to a minimum, with renewable input where possible.
- Electrical and Wi-Fi installation designed to minimize risks from electro-magnetic fields. Smoke alarms, carbon monoxide detectors essential and CO_2 detection if possible.
- Expert advice from architects, engineers and others to be free of their egotistical aims and based on listening to the buildings' users and creative collaboration.

References

1. https://accordgroup.org.uk/news/2020-10-02/construction-starts-on-uks-first-development-of-plastic-free-homes
2. Tom Woolley, *Building Materials, Health and Indoor Air Quality* (Routledge, 2017).

3. A. Bocco Guaneri, *Vegetarian Architecture* (Jovis Verlag, 2020).
4. https://www.10best.com/interests/explore/10-fascinating-facts-about-hobbiton-that-you-never-knew/university
5. https://www.theguardian.com/society/2021/aug/01/converted-offices-pose-deadly-risk-in-heatwaves-experts-warn
6. 'Climate Change 2021: The Physical Science Basis: Summary for Policy Makers', August 2021, at ipcc.ch/report/ar6/wg1
7. globaljustice.org.uk/our-campaigns/trade/corporate-courts/
8. https://eos.org/articles/banned-cfc-emissions-tracked-to-eastern-china
9. https://www.tcpa.org.uk/pages/category/healthy-homes-act
10. Ben Fogle, *Inspire: Life Lessons from the Wilderness* (William Collins, 2020).
11. https://www.grandviewresearch.com/industry-analysis/glamping-market
12. https://www.thousandhuts.org/
13. https://reforestingscotland.org/
14. http://www.oneplanetcouncil.org.uk/
15. https://ecologicalland.coop/
16. https://cohousing.org.uk/
17. http://www.communitylandtrusts.org.uk/
18. https://ecologicalland.coop/furzehill
19. https://earthbound.report/2021/02/05/irelands-greenest-community-cloughjordan-ecovillage/
20. https://www.theguardian.com/world/2018/aug/10/paradise-lost-what-happened-to-irelands-model-eco-village
21. https://lammas.org.uk/en/welcome-to-lammas/
22. https://lammas.org.uk/en/research/
23. https://ecovillage.org/
24. https://www.onecommunityglobal.org/overview/
25. https://www.thelandmagazine.org.uk/
26. https://www.accesstoland.eu/The-Irish-Regenerative-Land-Trust-IRLT
27. https://www.nweurope.eu/projects/project-search/shicc-sustainable-housing-for-inclusive-and-cohesive-cities/

Chapter Two

BUILDING WITH EARTH

Why Use Earth for Building?

Clay-bearing earth is an abundant material for construction and even today much of the world's population lives in earthen buildings. Earth buildings can be hand-crafted on site but earth-based products can also be prefabricated and delivered to site. There are a wide range of techniques including rammed earth, adobe (or mud brick), cob and (com)pressed earth brick for walling, earth floors, earth-based plasters and a range of composite products including clay such as wattle and daub, or clay mixed with straw or hemp or other natural fibres or mineral aggregates to give products of varying densities and end uses. Unfired earth materials provide an opportunity to use very low embodied-energy solutions, but some fired earth products are also discussed here due to their useful properties as their raw materials may be considered natural in origin.

It is normal for ground to be excavated for foundations and this can yield subsoil that may be suitable for building. Very stony ground is not ideal, but layers of clay and sand can sometimes be suitable. Building with earth that is imported from many miles away is not the most sustainable approach but this may be the only practical solution if you want to use unfired earth and do not have anything suitable on site, and any alternative has higher embodied energy.

Earth plasters can be particularly beautiful and used with a wide range of substrates, not just earthen structures. Earth is environmentally positive due to its low embodied energy and its many thermal and health-giving properties. The latter come about by the humidity-regulating effects of hygroscopic clay. The non-toxicity of the earthen minerals and earth building has positive thermal properties due to its thermal mass. On the other hand, synthetic plastic insulation has

Earth wall in house in Fifeshire, Scotland. (Photo: Becky Little)

been added to some earth buildings in the UK to meet building regulations and has led to problems of damp, mould and rot. Some earth techniques allow considerable scope for artistic expression as many organic shapes can be achieved, but earth can also fit in with a modern and even high-tech architectural style.

There are many existing earth buildings, mainly cob, in certain areas of the UK and Ireland, Devon and the midlands of Ireland for instance. Some cob buildings have been so badly renovated over the years with cement renders that their owners may not realize they are living in an earth building. Cement renders entrap moisture and damage the substrate but technical awareness and historic listing by the authorities mean that genuine cob and lime materials have to be used when renovating such buildings. Local expertise is strongest in Devon because of the need to renovate and restore cob houses in that region. (1)

What Sort of Earth?

A wide range of earth can be used for building. Clay is the smallest soil particle and it forms the binder for earthen materials. Organic-bearing materials such as topsoil for growing vegetables and compost is not suitable, but clay containing subsoils with some silt, sand and even stone aggregates to some extent are often found to be suitable, and the tests for suitability are relatively simple. A natural subsoil can be modified for building use by adding clay, sand or gravels as required.

Cob

Cob or 'lump' buildings are made of clay subsoil mixed with some straw; a little water can be added in by treading with the feet or using a digger. To see if the cob mixture is of the right consistency a small ball of the material should be rolled in the hand: if it is too dry it will fall apart and if too wet it will squash down. Cob is placed into the wall by hand, built up in layers and trodden down, though again the placing can also be done with a digger. Cob walls are traditionally built off a stone or brick plinth, preferably self-draining, and are quite wide, often about 600mm, but the walls may be thicker at the foot and narrower as they go higher. It is normal to protect cob walls from heavy rain as they are being constructed and there are many different tools and techniques to shape and form the walls. Windows, doors and wall plates are built in as work proceeds and the walls can be shaped in many ways. Cob has to be one of the most

sculptural of building materials as a wide range of shapes can be created. Walls are finished with clay or lime plasters and renders. It's important for there to be good roof overhangs to protect the walls from rain erosion. Apart from a host of books on cob building there are several places that run training courses in the UK and Ireland. (2) (3) (4)

Buildings have also been built from sods cut from the ground and stacked up in a similar way to cob or mud bricks. Many sod houses were built in the US and Canada in the nineteenth century but this method is less common today.

Cob devotees will argue that solid cob walls provide good thermal comfort and there is no doubt that the thermal mass of cob acts as a thermal flywheel,

Interior of cob house under construction. (Photo: The Hollies)

Constructing a cob wall. (Photo: The Hollies)

Living room in cob house, with stove. (Photo: the Hollies)

moderating temperature swings and thereby retaining heat in winter or keeping a building cool in summer. Cob houses were always heated with an open fire or stove in earlier times and the fire would have been kept alight all day in cooler weather. Animals could also have been bedded down in farmhouses to help with the warmth. Cob walls do not readily meet the thermal insulation standards required by modern building regulations and this has led to a number of experiments to add additional layers for insulation. Some cob buildings have been constructed with an extra external layer of polystyrene but this has led to dampness and is not to be recommended. An innovative design in Devon combining cob and strawbale seems a much more intelligent solution and others have tried lower-density cob using low-density mineral aggregates or bio-based aggregates such as extra straw, wood shavings, hemp shiv or miscanthus (a bamboo-like grass), or in conjunction with hempcrete. Working with mud is great fun and many argue that it is therapeutic as well as an opportunity to create very organic buildings.

If you are planning to build with cob it is essential to learn from experienced 'cobbers'. There are several centres that run cob building courses. The Hollies in West Cork in southern Ireland has twenty years' experience of building cob buildings and running courses and has an excellent website. (5) Cob was one of the very few materials available to poor people in Ireland and there were many thousands of cob houses still in use in the twentieth century, but misguided official grant schemes have led to the demolition of these earth houses and their replacement by structures with concrete block walls and PVC windows.

CobBauge Project

Staff at Plymouth University are involved in an EU-funded project to find ways to enable cob walls to meet building regulations using natural materials: this is known as the CobBauge Project. They have teamed up with French and UK partners, including Earth Building UK and Ireland (EBUKI), with EU funding.

(6) Their proposal involves a composite 600mm-thick wall, half of which is a conventional earth and straw cob mix with the other 50 per cent as a lightweight mixture of hemp and a clay slip. They have built two full-scale test walls and are starting to build a prototype classroom building on the Plymouth University campus. They claim that this composite will meet UK building regulations with a U value of 0.26W/m²K. At first sight it would seem impractical to have such a thick wall in most buildings but the initial study created even thicker walls. Such walls would have the additional benefit of excellent thermal mass and the health properties of using natural materials. Strawbale and even hempcrete walls can easily be 500mm thick, and rammed earth even thicker. This provides an option for those cob enthusiasts who want to use clay subsoil, where it is available, and creates a very low embodied-energy solution that will also meet the thermal standards in the building regulations. The partners have been carrying out extensive scientific tests of the structural and thermal properties and their

CobBauge Project at Plymouth University, test wall. (Photo: Jim Carfrae)

data is published and available from the project website or from the University of Plymouth. They would be willing to provide technical advice to self-builders and architects who might want to explore this as an option.

Other techniques, using cob-type mixtures, include earth bags and long thin bags filled with clay, looking rather like sausages, developed by German earth-building expert Gernot Minke (7); also see the Earthbag Village (8) and CalEarth in the US. (9)

Unfired Earth Bricks and Blocks and Adobe

Adobe or mud brick construction, making unfired earth bricks and blocks, is used all over the world. Mixing earth, clay, sand and straw in forms or machines, usually built into walls with a clay-based mortar, is a highly sustainable and efficient way to create buildings. While this may seem to be a technology more appropriate for developing countries, unfired earth bricks are made in the UK to a limited extent and they are widely used in drier areas of the US. While you might not want to build a house out of unfired bricks they may be useful as an internal wall to provide thermal mass or a decorative feature. They can be made in different densities to give different insulation performance and are easily incorporated into cob buildings. Hand-made unfired bricks can be seen as a form of rammed earth.

Will Stanwix has made a range of unfired earth bricks at H.G. Matthews Ltd, a company which specializes in handmade bricks. (10) Stanwix, who now runs the Hemp Block Company Ltd, has constructed a number of buildings using unfired bricks. As there are very few unfired earth brickmakers in the UK, you could have a go at making your own bricks if you have a suitable supply of clay, sand and straw.

The clay and straw mixture is pressed into simple moulds, the moulds removed and the bricks allowed to dry. Air-drying bricks in what used to be the UK's cool, damp climate is not easy but as we get hotter summers it may become similar to making bricks in Africa!

Village nursery, Bellingdon, near Chesham in Buckinghamshire, showing cob and brick walls. (Photo: Will Stanwix)

Laying cob bricks with hempcrete blocks. (Photo: Will Stanwix)

Rammed Earth

Substantial structural walls can be created from rammed earth. This is very different from cob and other handmade earth-based materials as the earth has to be compressed, usually using a mechanical form of compaction. This technique is unlikely to be readily available to self-builders on small projects but can be used on large projects where the cost of shuttering and mechanical processes can be met. Rammed earth walls provide a low embodied-energy alternative to concrete and create a much

Panoramic view of Holland Park Eco Centre rammed earth wall. (Photo: Rowland Keable)

more environmentally friendly solution for building thermal mass masonry walls. There is plenty of academic literature advocating the addition of cement to rammed earth, but this is not necessary and opposed by ecological earth builders. Rammed earth walls have been made in prefabricated form for domestic situations such as fireplaces and prefabricated walls. There is a factory making rammed earth products in Voralberg in Austria. (11) (12) (13)

Most rammed earth structures in the UK have been constructed on site, such as the Holland Park Eco Centre in West London. Opened in 2013, the building is a base for the Kensington and Chelsea Ecology Service and is an environmental education and biodiversity centre. It is a significant rammed earth ecological building in the heart of London. (14) Information is available from the builder, Rowland Keable of Rammed Earth Consulting. (15) Keable is a key member of the earth-building community in the UK and an expert on rammed earth, though much of his work is outside the UK: he has helped to write an important code of practice for rammed earth construction in Africa, as well as design and construction guidelines for the UK. (16)

The construction material for the Holland Park Centre was a grey brick clay mixed with red crushed limestone. The 50 tonnes of material were constructed in ten days in sub-zero temperatures with the materials brought to site in bags; they were then

Rammed earth wall under construction at Holland Park Eco Centre. (Photo: Rowland Keable)

Close-up view of rammed earth wall at Holland Park Eco Centre. (Photo: Nicola Kench)

mixed and taken to their final position in buckets and barrows and placed into shuttering. Photographs of the process can be viewed on Facebook. Another

Rammed earth wall at Holland Park, showing roof overhang.
(Photo: Nicola Kench)

Earth wall under construction in Berlin office, with heating pipes.
(Photo: ZRS Architects)

celebrated rammed earth wall can be found in the Wales Institute of Sustainable Education (WISE) building at the Centre for Alternative Technology in Wales. (17)

Earth Walls in Modern Architecture

It is common for modern architects in Germany to use earth wall products in their buildings. As well as carrying out conservation work to the many earth buildings still standing in Germany, earth plasters and walls are used to improve the indoor air quality in newbuild structures. (18)

Fired Bricks and Products

The majority of houses in the UK were built with fired bricks at one time. Using locally sourced clay is a reasonably natural way to build, though the energy used to fire bricks means that they do not have low embodied energy, unless, arguably, the kilns are fired using waste timber. Today bricks are shipped around the country, increasing transport costs, as many local brickworks have shut down. Excellent information and advice about bricks can be obtained from the Brick Development Association (19) and it can be seen immediately by looking at their membership list how few brick companies now exist in the UK.

Some are mainly concrete block companies as well as making bricks.

Brick Slips

As you travel around England in particular, large swathes of green belt appear to be being swallowed up by tightly packed developments from the mainstream housing developers, following a rather predictable kitschy neo-vernacular style with brick facades. These houses are invariably timber frame with brick slips stuck to the outside with adhesive. Brick slips are like tiles that are sometimes cut from full bricks (with the rest thrown away) or specially made in various thicknesses and then fired. Some multi-storey buildings use prefabricated metal panels with brick slips or tiles as cladding.

The natural builder will probably not want to use stick-on bricks though they could be attached to a hempcrete wall or used in some form of rainscreen cladding, especially where the local planning permission requires a brick finish to match in with the local vernacular. However, traditional fired bricks may be useful as a form of rainscreen cladding in conjunction with natural insulations. Second-hand bricks recovered from demolition might be an option but these can be hard to find and very expensive.

Poroton Hollow Bricks

One of the largest companies that owns much of the UK brick and roof tile production is the Austrian multinational Wienerberger. Wienerberger are one of the leading companies that produce Poroton hollow bricks which are widely used throughout Europe. There are numerous other hollow clay block or 'ziegel' manufacturers in Europe but Wienerberger are the main supplier in the UK with their Porotherm product. The hollow clay blocks are glued

together with mortar, which is a quick and easy way to construct walls. In order to meet thermal performance requirements, additional insulation is normally required as well as an external render coat for weather protection.

Despite the widespread use of hollow clay blocks in Europe, they have never been very popular in the UK, though there have been a number of small-scale schemes using the technique in Bristol, Norfolk and Leicestershire and they are promoted as a way to create 'healthy housing' using the Wienerberger E4

Housing development in England under construction using Porotherm blocks. (Photo: Wienerberger)

Laying Porotherm blocks with mortar bed. (Photo: Wienerberger)

system. The system involves a brick outer leaf and an insulated cavity using plastic foam PIR (polyisocyanurate) insulation. (20) Some Poroton bricks are also supplied with the cavities filled with mineral wool insulation.

Earthships

There a few enthusiasts who advocate a form of construction called 'earthships'. This involves constructing walls of used car tyres which are then rammed full of earth, with an earth or cement plaster layer being used to cover the tyres. The earthship idea was developed in Arizona and New Mexico in the US, and there are a handful of earthship buildings in the UK and Europe. Earthships are highly controversial because of concern about creating walls from a highly toxic material. Tyres are responsible for significant particle pollution as they are made with a cocktail of chemicals including 6PPD, PAHs (pyrene and phenanthrene), benzothiazoles, phenols, bisphenols, dimethylebutyl, toluene, arsenic and acetone, plus a combination of metals and carbon black. Earthship devotees argue that tyres do not emit toxic chemicals as they are stable when in a building, and that in any case the earth plaster will prevent this even though earth plasters are breathable. Using tyres outside a building such as in foundations (*see* Chapter 5 on straw bales) may be a useful way to recycle a tiny number of used tyres, however. There are other projects known as 'earthhouses' that also advocate the use of tyres in the walls, floors and roofs of a building, so the occupants would be completely surrounded by tyres. There is significant evidence of a cancer risk from the widespread use of rubber crumb from tyres, which is used on sportsfields and children's playgrounds and is even used in artificial turf. The debate will continue about potential emissions from car tyres in walls but applying the precautionary principle it might be best to avoid this. (21)

Earth Floors

It's possible to create very attractive floors from natural earth. The build-up of the subfloor is critical and building a successful earth floor is quite a specialized task using a breathable aggregate base made from stone or recycled glass insulation. The earth is often built up in layers using materials much the same as in cob construction, then the earth is plastered or polished, oiled, buffed and possibly waxed. Alternatively, adobe bricks can be laid in a stiff mud-brick mortar bed. Self-builders can do this themselves but there are also specialist companies that can supply materials. Current prices range from £140 to £380 per square metre. There is an American earth floor material called Claylin which may be available in UK and Ireland. Underfloor heating pipes can be placed in an earth floor but it needs sufficient time to dry out. The oil used to seal the floor is normally tung and linseed which can be regarded as creating VOC emissions, but these are natural oils. There are differing views about whether it is alright to lay an earth floor on top of an impermeable plastic membrane as a radon barrier or waterproof layer, but this has been done successfully. (22) (23)

Earth Plasters

Earth plasters and clay-based paints provide a wonderful way to finish the interior of a natural building. Clay plasters can go onto strawbale and hempcrete walls as well as earth walls. Clay plasters can be made and applied by self-builders but there are also very sophisticated professional materials and plasterers offering high-end finishes at high-end prices. However, if you want to mix your own plaster you will probably need to mix three buckets of sand to one of clay, plus chopped straw or other vegetable matter (and/or cellulose fibre from pulped paper) and wheat paste. A bucket of fresh cow manure comes in useful. There are many recipes. It may

Becky Little in front of earth-plastered wall. (Photo: Becky Little)

Earth-plastered wall showing range of possible finishes.
(Photo: Becky Little)

Earth wall under construction using adobe bricks and earth
mortar. (Photo: Becky Little)

Earth wall with clay plaster, completed. (Photo: Becky Little)

be necessary to screen out stones and not add too much water. Applying the plaster, once you have the right consistency, can be a satisfying and therapeutic experience.

One of the most inspiring earth builders in the UK is Becky Little. Based in Fife in Scotland, she carries out earth-building and plastering work but also runs training workshops:

At Rebearth we strive to create forms and finishes that are beautiful, ecological and health-giving. In collaboration with architects and designers we work with natural materials to create hand-crafted bespoke structures and surfaces. This creative work is wide in scope, from highly finished objects and decorative plaster to earth-built furniture and construction. As well as integrating buildings and art we are constantly developing new techniques that innovate from tradition. We can work to a commission or collaborate to develop an idea, from materials sourcing and testing to site build. Recent projects have included a community mudwall shelter, thermally efficient earth mixes in homes and offices, research and development of sculptural and acoustic clay plasters, and polished clay balls. (24)

Some manufactured clay plasters require a reinforcing mesh which can be a natural fibre such as hessian and flax but some companies also offer glass fibre. Great claims are made for the health and ecological benefits of clay and earth plasters but this is not necessarily correct if the finishes are applied to less ecological materials. Ideally, clay materials should be used with other ecological materials including clay boards and other vapour-permeable materials. A range of manufactured products are available which come in bags and you just need to add water.

Clayworks project, interior. (Photo: Matt Austin)

Clayworks project, detail. (Photo: Matt Austin)

Clayworks plaster in Scottish glamping cabin.
(Photo: Clayworks)

as advisory sections on strawbale, light earth method and straw/clay. NZS 4298 also has sections on the testing of earthen materials for suitability.

The standards cover earth building materials, strength, durability, fire resistance, reinforcement, foundations, structural strength and much more. This highly professional and thorough suite of standards should provide a model for those who advocate standards for other natural materials in addition to timber and timber products which are reasonably well covered. There may even come a day when BSI (British Standards Institute) and ISO (International Organization for Standardization) standards exist for natural materials, though such standards only come about when industry or government agencies are willing to fund the work. There are also US standards for earth building systems, including ASTM E2392 / E2392M-10(2016). (25)

Earth Building Standards

Earth building is not well represented in UK regulations and standards, like so many other natural materials, and so projects have to be argued through on a case-by-case basis. In New Zealand, on the other hand, earth building standards have been adopted by the government thanks to the work of Graeme North and other natural builders. Of particular importance in New Zealand and other countries where earth building is common or popular is the issue of earthquakes and so it has been necessary to agree seismic standards for earth construction.

Standards have existed for earth building in New Zealand since 1998. These have now been extensively revised. The New Zealand Earth Building Standards NZS 4297, NZS 4298 and NZS 4299:2020 have new sections on lower-density earthen materials, earth floors, plasters and internal adobe veneers, as well

Selected Manufacturers of Clay Plaster Products

Tierrafino (The Netherlands but with stockists in the UK and Ireland) (26)
Claytec (several stockists in the UK) (27)
H.G. Matthews Ltd (28)
Clayworks (Cornwall) (29)
Safran (Estonia) (30)

There is a very useful reference book by Weisman and Bryce with the self-explanatory title *Clay and Lime Renders, Plasters and Paint*. (31)

Will Stanwix's office: timber frame infilled with light clay and straw blocks. (Photo: Will Stanwix)

Earth plastering in progress. (Photo: Will Stanwix)

The pleasure of applying earth plaster. (Photo: Will Stanwix)

References

1. https://www.devonearthbuilding.com/index.htm
2. Becky Bee, *The Cob Builders Handbook: You Can Hand-Sculpt Your Own Home* (Groundworks, 1990).
3. John McCann, *Clay and Cob Buildings* (Shire, 1983).

4. Adam Weismann and Katy Bryce, *Building with Cob: A Step-by-Step Guide* (Green Books, 2006).
5. https://www.thehollies.ie/
6. http://www.cobbauge.eu/en/
7. Gernot Minke, *Building with Earth: Design and Technology of a Sustainable Architecture* (Birkhauser, 2012).
8. https://www.onecommunityglobal.org/earthbag-village/
9. https://www.calearth.org/
10. https://www.hgmatthews.com/
11. https://www.lehmtonerde.at/en/
12. Martin Rauch, *Refined Earth: Construction and Design with Rammed Earth* (Detail Special, 2015).
13. Anna Heringer, Lindsay Blair Howe and Martin Rauch, *Upscaling Earth: Material, Process, Catalyst* (gta Verlag, 2019).
14. https://www.rbkc.gov.uk/environment/holland-park-ecology-centre/
15. http://rammedearthconsulting.com/rammed-earth-holland-park-eco-centre.htm
16. Peter Walker, Rowland Keable, Joe Martin, Vasilios Maniatidis, *Rammed Earth: Design and Construction Guidelines* (IHS BRE Press, 2005).
17. https://cat.org.uk/info-resources/free-information-service/building/the-wise-building/
18. https://www.zrs.berlin/project/conservation-and-rehabilitation-of-a-cob-building-in-leipzig-losnig-germany/
19. https://www.brick.org.uk/
20. https://www.wienerberger.co.uk/content/dam/wienerberger/united-kingdom/marketing/documents-magazines/brochures/UK_MKT_DOC_Wienerberger_e4_Brick_House_Brochure.pdf
21. http://hackingtheearthship.blogspot.com/2015/01/tire-off-gassing-research.html
22. http://earthfloors.co.uk/contact
23. Sukita Reay Crimmel and James Thomson, *Earthen Floors: A Modern Approach to an Ancient Practice* (New Society Publishers, 2014).
24. https://www.rebearth.co.uk/work/project-two-49zf8
25. https://www.astm.org/Standards/E2392.htm
26. http://www.tierrafino.co.uk/
27. https://www.claytec.de/en/products/clay-plaster#
28. https://www.hgmatthews.com/lime-and-cob/earth-mortars-renders/powdered-clay/
29. https://clay-works.com/
30. https://www.safran.ee/plasters-pastes/2016/8/19/clay-plaster
31. Adam Weismann and Katy Bryce, *Clay and Lime Renders, Plasters and Paints: A How-To Guide to Using Natural Finishes* (Green Books, 2015).

Chapter Three

TIMBER

At Mole [Architects] we have long seen timber as the perfect constructional material; low in embodied energy, easy to transport, forgiving to work with, and suited to quick and clean construction. We have worked with most forms of 'modern methods of construction' (MMC), from our first building using prefabricated panelised cassettes to recent buildings made from cross-laminated timber (CLT) sheets. Timber absorbs CO_2 during its growth, and as long as this is locked up in a building it is of environmental benefit. There's a beauty in natural materials that is hard to replicate, and we love the fact that for all the technical advances in timber production, we still simply love the smell of cedar, the figured beauty of Douglas fir, or the richness of a piece of cherry. (1)

Timber is the pre-eminent natural material and will be a mainstay of any natural building. Timber can be used as the main structure but also for much of the internal fitting out and finishes. While all timber is natural, there are a wide range of composite and processed timber materials that can be used, though some are more sustainable and ecological than others.

Using timber is a sustainable way to construct buildings and has many benefits, particularly ease of construction, flexibility and recyclability. Timber, providing it has not been treated with toxic chemicals, helps to ensure healthy comfortable buildings and many people find wood therapeutic, creating a softer gentler environment. Timber can create beautiful buildings through structure and finishes.

The world's forests are crucial for the survival of biodiversity and reduction of CO_2 and there is much talk of planting millions of trees by governments and voluntary organizations. While this is to be welcomed, timber for construction relies on trees that were planted decades or even centuries ago. The UK

Timber house in Scotland. (Photo: Adam Gillingham)

has very little woodland, however, and has largely relied on timber imported from North America and the Baltic for construction. The UK is one of the least wooded areas of Europe, with just 11.7 per cent woodland cover compared to around 37 per cent for the EU. Northern Ireland has just 6.5 per cent, followed by England at 8.7 per cent. (2)

Home-grown timber, planted by the Forestry Commission and large landowners, has been generally of poor-quality quick-growing spruce and is used for processed wood products. Much of it was planted for paper production and fence posts. There is some certified slower-grown softwood which can be used in building, particularly from Ireland, and there are limited amounts of hardwood, much of which is used as 'green' timber. Green and roundwood timber is popular with natural builders and reduces dependence on imported commercial timber. (Roundwood is wood in its natural state as felled, with or without bark.)

Managing forests sustainably involves felling or thinning of trees and some of this wood can be used in buildings. Specialist sawmills exist in some parts of the UK, such as the New Forest (3) and the Forest of Dean for example, but there are many more. (4) The Welsh government has been active in promoting the use of Welsh timber, and organizations like Wood Knowledge Wales are active in promoting the use of local timber for construction. (5) It is worth searching for local sources of timber and methods of construction that will make the best use of this important resource. A useful overview of a wide range of issues relating to sustainable and local timber was conducted by Ivor Davies of Napier University and CAT (Centre for Alternative Technology), and this was published by the Forestry Commission in 2016. (6)

Certified Timber

Much of the timber from local builders or timber merchants is likely to have been imported from Canada, the US, the Baltic, South East Asia and Africa. If you have ethical and environmental concerns then you will need to do some research to check the source of the timber and whether you are happy to buy it if you cannot source locally grown and sawn timber. There can be barriers to local timber use as it may not be stress-graded and certified as from a sustainable source.

The main certification of timber is by the Forest Stewardship Council (FSC). (7) This international scheme came from very radical and ethical roots but over the years appears to have become more and more commercial. One recent venture is to certify Pirelli tyres: these contain certified natural rubber from FSC-certified plantations which are then used on BMW hybrid cars, but the tyres also contain many dangerous and toxic synthetic and organic additives. FSC governance has representatives from the timber industry but also includes many environmentalists. You may find the FSC logo stamped on timber bought from your local timber merchant. The other certification label on wood may be from PEFC (Programme for the Endorsement of Forest Certification) (8). PEFC began as a purely commercial timber industry-run body but tries to look more like FSC; its governance through its board, while including environmentalists, still seems weighted towards industry people.

Locally grown timber, from a local sawmill, may be managed sustainably (even if it doesn't have certification), whereas if it is coming from across the world, how confident are you that the certification is genuine? There can be quite a bit of confusion about the sustainability of timber and some is sold as from 'well-managed or sustainable forests' without any proof of this. Timber in North America is still being clear-felled or harvested without certification. Western red cedar, which is very popular with architects for cladding, is marketed as sustainable but may not actually be certified by FSC or PEFC. Western red cedar is an endangered species, and also affected by disease, and yet it is still being used by the construction industry in large amounts.

Timber and Fire Safety

As a result of the Grenfell Inquiry the construction industry has become much more risk-averse, with the UK government introducing stricter regulation about health and safety and fire risks. However, bizarrely, this has impacted on the use of timber construction, even though wood was not a factor in the Grenfell deaths. Changes to building regulations or policies may make it more difficult to use engineered timber and timber cladding (though this is less likely to affect domestic buildings). Concerns about fire in buildings has given a boost to cement and concrete when it should have focussed on minimizing the use of flammable plastic materials.

A huge growth in fires in low-rise apartments in recent years has led to a ban by some house builders on using wooden balconies, even though there is little evidence that this a major factor in house fires. Timber cladding has also been lumped together with plastic flammable materials even though it need not be as great a risk. Unfortunately, much commercial timber frame construction continues to use flammable plastic insulation materials. (9) (10) (11)

Solid timber such as cross-laminated panels and thick posts and beams and roundwood timber are reasonably safe in fire as timber chars. As a general rule, the thinner the timber member the greater the fire risk.

Timber Costs and Burning Wood

Anyone who has been buying timber for construction in recent times will have noticed a shocking increase in prices. Stress-graded softwood, plywood and many other products are much more expensive than was the case in the past. The global demand for timber has skyrocketed since the world went into lockdown, with prices increasing by up to 130 per cent since 2019. Stock market valuations of timber have increased by 375 per cent. A commitment to lower carbon construction and healthier buildings has led to an increase in demand but costs of all construction materials have also increased. (12) Despite this problem, this should not put natural builders off the idea of using timber for construction but it is worth considering ways to use wood more effectively, waste as little as possible and look for alternative sources.

Burning wood should be restricted to waste offcuts and fallen trees but the UK government heavily subsidizes wood instead of coal for electricity production, leading to the importation of wood pellets from the US. Long trains heading to Drax power station from Liverpool docks can be seen bringing pellets from the US (13) and it has been suggested that this is leading to the clear-felling of valuable forests. (14)

The use of wood pellets in Northern Ireland, through an overly generous Renewable Heat Incentive scheme, became a national scandal and led to the collapse of the Stormont Assembly. (15) Ten million tonnes of wood waste is sent to landfill every year in the UK. (16) Clearly, wood is still not treated as the valuable resource that it should be. (17)

Most primary school children know that trees are essential to life as they absorb carbon dioxide and release oxygen and yet there has been a debate about the usefulness of trees as part of CO_2 mitigation. It is useful to know that you are not destroying the planet if you use timber in your natural building and that you are locking up carbon in the structure rather than creating CO_2 emissions from the use of cement and concrete. Timber has to be constantly replanted and thinned: this process is essential to biodiversity while benefiting our overall health. Much timber is owned by the agroforest industry but there are a growing number of small woodland owners (18) and co-operative, community and social enterprise woodland projects and in the long term these may be useful sources of timber supply for natural builders. The Donegal Woodland Owners Society in Ireland is a great example of how small woodland owners collaborate to share machinery and market their wood. (19)

Ways of Building with Wood

Roundwood Timber

It is possible to source roundwood poles from sawmills in some parts of the UK and Ireland. Poles are normally cleaned of bark and should have been seasoned. Oak, beech, larch, Douglas fir and other species may be suitable. You can create structures of poles and beams using roundwood timber which can create a very strong structure. Roundwood timber is stronger than machined rectangular sections of timber as it has the inherent strength of the timber.

Many eco builders like to create round buildings, for which roundwood timber is suitable, and specially to create a reciprocal roof. Such roofs can be very strong, using interlocking poles, and can be constructed without the need for much scaffolding or temporary supports. There are many guides, YouTube videos and books which will show you how to do this. A good one to start with would be Tony Wrench's *A Simple Round House Manual* (20).

Roundwood timber provides excellent structural properties for timber frame construction for both uprights and roof timbers.

Reciprocal roof at the Down to Earth training building, South Wales. (Photo: Down to Earth)

Reciprocal roof at Lough Mardal holiday village, main building. (Photo: Marcus Tindal)

Roundwood timber posts and framing at Lough Mardal holiday village. (Photo: Marcus Tindal)

Whole Woods training building near Lampeter, Ceredigion, showing reciprocal roof. (Photo: Tŷ Pren)

Tŷ Pren's roundwood frame for bunkhouse at Fordhall Community Farm, near Market Drayton, Shropshire; strawbale walls constructed later by others. (Photo: Tŷ Pren)

Species	Available with FSC/PEFC?
Greenheart	
Opepe	
Ekki	
Purpleheart	
Keruing	
Balau	
Basralocus	
Kapur	
Green oak	
Douglas fir	
Larch	
Pitch pine	
Siberian larch	FSC
Walnut	
Utile	
Tulipwood	FSC
Burma teak	
Sapele	FSC
Southern yellow pine	

Species	Available with FSC/PEFC?
Quebec yellow pine	FSC
Parana pine	
White oak	
Red oak	
European oak	FSC
Seraya	
Majau	PEFC
Rock maple	
Iroko	
Hemlock	
Idigbo/Emery	
Cherry	
Western red cedar	
Brazilian cedar	
West African mahogony	
Steamed beech	PEFC
Ash	
Agba	
Afrormosia	

Table 3.1
Timber stock list from the website of Gilmour & Aitken, Alexandria, West Dumbartonshire, Scotland. (21)

Hardwood Timber

Most timber construction uses imported pine soft-wood but it is also possible to use hardwood. Local hardwood from UK and Ireland can be obtained from local sawmills and consists mainly of oak and ash. Elm was used a great deal in the past but there are very few elm trees left. Some species of ash are badly affected by disease and many are being cut down so there may be good-quality ash available in the short term. Oak and ash structural timbers, flooring, doors and other elements will lend beauty and character to buildings. Other wood such as birch, sycamore, beech, walnut, chestnut and many more may not be suitable for structural elements but can still be used for finishes inside.

Tropical hardwoods may be seen as unethical as there has been so much publicity about illegal logging and the destruction of rainforests. Much of the clearance in places like the Amazon basin has been to create space for soya growing and cattle farms rather than just for the timber industry. In the Far East the clearance has been to create space for palm oil plantations. On the other hand, there are countries in Africa and Asia where tropical hardwood is managed sustainably and responsibly and has FSC certification. Some tree thinning is necessary and tropical hardwoods from fair trade and sustainable communities can be obtained in the UK, but it is important to carefully check out the sources and credibility of any certification. The market for such tropical hardwood helps sustain poor communities and encourages the people in the area to respect and look after their forests but it's crucial to check with the supplier the authenticity of such information. Table 3.1 gives an indication of the wide range of species available from one merchant though only a minority have FSC certification and this list may not be up to date.

Softwoods

Douglas fir, larch, pine and spruce can be used to create timber structures and some of it may be from local sources. Sawn softwood from your local timber and builders' merchant will nearly always be imported, however. Timber is graded and you will come across reference to C16 and C24, though there are twelve strength grades (BS 5268). The grading is for what is generally referred to as carcassing timber. Both C16 and C24 can be used for wall plates, rafters, floor joists, studs and so on. C24 is stronger.

The moisture content is also a key factor and timber should be at 20 per cent or lower, though you will notice that a lot of softwood timber is stored outside in merchants' yards and can be soaking wet when you get it. Timber will dry down to 12 per cent moisture content and this can result in some shrinkage. As a result there can be movement inside timber frames once constructed.

Fast-growing timber from spruce plantations planted over many years by the UK Forestry Commission is generally too weak for structural use and is generally used for fencing, fence posts, pallets and so on. The slower the growth of the timber the stronger it is and many forests in Scandinavia and the Baltic states have been sustainably managed by families and co-operatives for hundreds of years. (22) Some slower-growth spruce may be suitable for construction, however.

Structural Advice

You may assume that it is relatively easy to construct a simple timber frame building without expert advice, but if you are to comply with the building regulations you may need to use the services of a structural engineer. While it is relatively simple to use timber joist span tables it is necessary to get an engineer to calculate racking, shear and wind resistance. Timber wall plates must be tied to the ground and floor loadings have to be justified. Diagonal bracing may be required. Package deal timber frame companies that provide panelized systems may seem like a cheap and easy solution but are not always suitable for the natural builder. These companies largely rely on composite boards fixed to the timber frame to provide racking resistance and the panels will also arrive wrapped in plastic breather membranes. If you want to build with strawbale or hempcrete this is not appropriate. Many timber frame companies will not diverge from their standard systems as this will invalidate their warranties.

Softwood Timber Treatment

The best way to season timber is to air-dry it but, given the speed of commercial timber turnover, much of the graded timber in your local merchant will have been kiln-dried. The timber drying process is conducted to reduce the moisture content and this will reduce the risk of warping, splitting and shrinkage as well as problems in processing machinery. Timber is stacked and dried in ovens for three to five days. The timber can also be heat-treated where the temperature of 56°C is maintained for at least thirty minutes.

Timber is also treated using a variety of chemicals such as copper as a preservative and fungicide. Copper chrome arsenic (CCA) was the most widely used treatment until it was banned in Europe as being far too toxic and carcinogenic. The timber is treated in a vacuum chamber where the air is extracted and then filled with chemicals which are absorbed by the wood. The market for timber treatment chemicals seems dominated by one US company, Osmose, who also own the Protim brand familiar in the UK. Treated timber is tinted with a yellow, green or brown colour which allows you to discriminate between it and untreated timber. The green dye makes the timber look as it has been treated with the illegal CCA. Chemicals used include m-phenoxbenzyl and dimethylcyclopropanecarboxylate (permethrin).

These chemicals are officially classified as dangerous for the environment and health and you are strongly advised to use gloves when handling treated timber over a period of time. Toxic chemicals are released when such wood is burned, which is frequently done to get rid of offcuts on building sites. Treated timber should never be used in stoves or open fires.

In the past timber posts were treated with creosote, which has also been banned as carcinogenic, though you will still see wooden telephone and electricity posts that have used creosote as this is still allowed in certain circumstances. Modern post treatments are generally stained brown to look like creosote and some give off the most awful chemical smell.

Many architects and builders seem to think that timber will begin to rot as soon as it goes into a building and prefer to use treated timber, even inside. It is normal to use treated timber for external roofing and cladding battens as they may be exposed to water, but untreated timber should be fine in a well-designed building as long as it remains dry and not subject to interstitial dampness. Unfortunately, much modern timber frame construction wraps everything in plastic and there can be risks of interstitial condensation which can affect timber. You will come across claims that emissions affecting indoor air quality from treated timber are minor but these are made by the Wood Protection Association, who promote the careful use of wood treatments. (23) It is important to realize that some timber is also treated with flame retardants which are also highly toxic endocrine disruptors, bad for human health.

Pickling Timber

Another form of timber treatment is using vinegar, a process known as acetylation or 'pickling', which is claimed to turn softwood into a hardwood. The vinegar, acetic anhydride, is used in what is best known under the brand name Accoya. The leading supplier of Accoya is based in Arnhem in The Netherlands, but it is also produced in New Zealand and elsewhere. While the process makes the timber more expensive, it is preferable to using normal toxic timber treatments. You can also treat your own timber using vinegar as this was done in the past to darken wood but this may be rather labour-intensive and will put you off fish and chips for life. (24)

Vinegar-treated timber painted with Osmo wood stain at the Rediscovery Centre, Ballymun, Dublin.

Post and Beam Construction

There are a growing number of companies that process UK-grown hardwood, such as oak and softwoods like Douglas fir and larch, for post and beam construction. There is a greater choice of good UK-grown timber available than a few years ago. Oak-framed buildings have become very fashionable and those who can afford it use oak frames in new houses. There are many specialist companies catering for the high-end 'bespoke' market. While oak-frame houses can be very beautiful many are built by companies that also use plastic non-natural insulation materials. Carpenter Oak, for instance, one of the longest-established companies, generally offer Warmcel cellulose insulation, but they also offer structural insulated panels (SIPs) using synthetic foam insulations with polyurethane or polystyrene insulation. (25) Despite the cost, oak frame package deals can be an attractive option and some companies offer a more affordable option using Douglas fir instead of oak. The Welsh Oak Frame company offer a useful guide to costs. The list below gives more examples.

Woodland Oak barn, showing frame under construction. (Photo: Peter Tebby)

Woodland Oak barn completed.
(Photo: Peter Tebby)

Timber frame at Abbey St Bathans, Berwickshire, with hempcrete walls in the background. (Photo: Charlotte Dobie)

Selected Oak Frame Companies

Carpenter Oak
Border Oak (26)
Oakwrights (27)
Oakmasters (28)
The Complete Oak Home (29)
West Wind Oak (30)
Prime Oak (31)
Julius Bahn (32)
Welsh Oak Frame (33)
Wye Oak (34)

Log Homes

Some self-builders and environ-mentalists are attracted by the idea that a 'log cabin' is an eco-logical solution for their house or building. Most so-called log cabins use imported wood from British Columbia or Scandinavian pine timber but very few log cabins are built from real logs. Some manu-factured log homes can even look as if they are made from plastic and some even use the term 'log effect' in their marketing. Some claim that their log cabins are eco homes but build with plastic foam insulation as they try to keep the walls very thin. (35) (36) Some also promote the idea that you do not need planning permission for log cabins because permitted develop-ment rules in planning policies may allow some in the back garden for leisure use, though not to live in.

Timber frame at Abbey St Bathans, with hempcrete walls. (Photo: Charlotte Dobie)

ModuLog holiday cabin with logs on the roof. (Photo: moduLog Celwood)

You could choose to buy roundwood logs and stack them on top of each other to create walls of a house using techniques pioneered on the west coast of the US and Canada. Some companies selling log cabins may use full real logs. (37) There are countless YouTube videos on the internet of people constructing log cabins from scratch in Alaska and British Columbia, as well as a host of TV shows, many of them showing scant regard for health and safety when using chainsaws, which is why they are not listed here!

An important thing to remember when using green logs, or even logs that have been well seasoned, is that there will be movement and shrinkage and this can lead to gaps and draughts. Early pioneers would stuff the cracks with straw, earth and clay. Log cabins sound romantic but have to be treated with caution.

Modern Methods of Construction Using Timber

Mainstream housing developers are increasingly using timber frames of various kinds for speculative housing. Frequently they clad the outside of the houses with brick slips so that they look like brick houses, or sometimes with render for a fake Georgian look. Profit-driven house builders try to find the cheapest possible ways to build though of course it is not suggested here that they cut corners as well!

The main problem with new timber frame building systems, usually referred to as modern methods of construction (MMC), is that they are very lightweight. There is no thermal mass in the houses and levels of insulation and airtightness may just meet the regulations but with a minimal thermal performance. Many houses suffer particularly from overheating, which has become a major problem, especially in the south of England. Skills in the construction industry are poor and so the houses underperform thermally but are also serious fire hazards. Not only do many builders use flammable plastic foam insulation materials, but flawed construction can allow for fire passages through the structure. Stephanie Barwise QC, an advisor to the Grenfell Inquiry, produced a report claiming a systemic nationwide problem of house builders failing to install cavity barriers.

Typical timber frame construction, showing airtightness membrane.

Cavity barriers are meant to stop the spread of fire through the building fabric, but even when installed correctly doubts remain about the efficacy of some systems. Following Barwise's report several housing developers have had to carry out extensive inspects of their recently built homes, with Persimmon Homes carrying out 500 inspections per week. (38)

This book is not about the many failures of mainstream modern methods of construction but if readers have the misfortune to live in one of these houses it's important to understand what is wrong with them and why natural building methods are so much better.

Composite modern methods of construction and structural insulation panel (SIP) houses are either constructed from prefabricated stud frame panels (panelized frames) which are lined with composite glued wood boards and plastic membranes, or from structural insulated panels in which lining boards are filled with foam insulation (SIPS). There are a range of so-called modular and volumetric house-building factories being set up with government support in an effort to meet demand for new housing: some companies use lightweight steel frames and others use recycled steel shipping containers for house construction.

Some stud frame panels are filled with mineral wool insulation, which may be less flammable, but SIPS are usually made with polyurethane (PUR) or polyisocyanurate (PIR) similar to the insulation behind the cladding on Grenfell, or polystyrene (EPS). While there will be greater restrictions on the use of flammable insulations on buildings over 18 metres in the future, the vast majority of houses and small blocks of flats in the UK are below 18 metres and so flammable insulations will continue to be used.

Prefabricated timber frame panels being loaded for transport to site. (Photo: Down to Earth)

Eco housing being constructed at Pennard in South Wales by Down to Earth. (Photo: Down to Earth)

Despite the use of timber frames, these houses also contain many chemical-based materials which may be responsible for long-lasting emissions and result in poor indoor air quality. It is possible to prefabricate timber frame houses using more environmentally friendly insulation materials as was done by Down to Earth at Pennard.

Engineered Timber Products

In addition to using simple sawn timber studs, posts, beams and joists there are a wide range of composite engineered timber products, some of which may be attractive to the natural and self-builder.

I-Beams

As solid timber becomes more expensive it is worth considering engineered products such as I-beams which are lighter than solid wood and can provide a greater span, while being easily lifted into place. While they can burn more easily than solid wood joists and rafters, they are always enclosed with plasterboard or other fireproof material and not left exposed inside the building. Such engineered products can be made with plywood or oriented strand board (OSB) and poorer-quality timber, thus reducing the impact on good-quality wood resources. Most of these engineered products rely on glues and unsurprisingly

the manufacturers claim that these should not cause serious emission problems. The industry has been working towards the use of low-emission adhesives.

Metal Web Joists

Composite timber joists with steel webs are available and you may be able to find a company in your area that can fabricate them to your needs. They can be used as uprights, rafters and in roof trusses and joists. (39)

Composite Boards and CLT

Plywood is familiar as the result of gluing timber together to create large boards but glued timber products can also include glulam joists and beams, and a less familiar product made in Finland called LVL (laminated veneer lumber). (40) Solid timber panels called cross-laminated timber (CLT), sometimes referred to as 'mass timber', are becoming more common. Made in Austria and Sweden, CLT is a quick way to prefabricate walls with a strong structural element that can be used in multi-storey or domestic buildings. CLT can be used with the finished wood face exposed inside a dwelling but with insulation and cladding added externally. (41) (42) CLT panels are sometimes covered with plasterboard and finished in the normal way. The panels are connected together and can be used as walls, floors and roofs. CLT panels are glued but there is a glue-free system called Brettstapel which uses wooden dowels. If you are interested in using Brettstapel it would be worth getting advice from Napier University in Edinburgh. (43)

Some CLT buildings have been constructed using plastic foam and mineral wool insulation but it is perfectly possible, and better, to use natural insulation boards such as wood fibre and this is quite common. Emissions from the glues in CLT are claimed to be very low but concerns may remain about the use of isocyanate and other chemical glues.

The huge insurance company Legal & General decided to set up a 51,000 square metre (550,000 square feet) factory in Yorkshire producing CLT panel houses, amid much fanfare, but production was very slow with large losses, and then a new managing director came in from Rolls Royce and changed the production to concrete and steel frame. It is not clear whether they are still producing CLT houses as well. (44)

Other CLT/mass timber companies in the UK include Eurban (45), Binderholz (46) and Stora Enso (47). KLH was contacted but refused to provide any information as they were 'too busy'.

Some excellent work was carried out around 2010–15 by an organization called Tŷ Unnos in Wales. They produced a range of composite wood products using Welsh timber and OSB, producing box beams,

ladder beams and diaphragm panels. This work was supported by Coed Cymru and some further work has done by builder Kenton Jones. (48) Some projects have been carried out using box beams and columns.

Interior CLT finished walls, Adderstone Crescent. (Photo: Eurban)

CLT house, 'Hollamby's', under construction. (Photo: Eurban)

Interior CLT walls, Janson's. (Photo: Eurban)

Vitsœ factory, Royal Leamington Spa, showing walls and roof using CLT.

Artist's studio finished with timber cladding. (Photo: Roger Mears)

Cambridge house with CLT walls and floors. (Photo: Mole Architects)

Tŷ Unnos box frame assembly in off-site factory. (Photo: Kenton Jones)

Tŷ Unnos box frame used for artist's studio, Ty Melinydd, Carmarthenshire. (Photo: Roger Mears)

Tŷ Unnos modular houses under construction with timber cladding. (Photo: Kenton Jones)

Shingles and Shakes

Timber roofing shingles are an ancient method of roofing using a natural material. Slate is a natural material but increasingly this is imported from across the world, for example from Spain and, increasingly, China. Cedar shingles are almost certainly imported and one of the main suppliers is a company that makes cement roofing tiles! English Woodlands Timber sells 'bias cut' shingles from oak wood sourced in France. Hand-split shakes can be found from UK companies but are usually imported from countries like Austria; various woods can be used, including oak, larch, white fir, robinia and spruce. (49) Even wooden gutters are available. Shingles can be made from sweet chestnut; there is a manufacturer in Gloucestershire. (50)

Timber Rainscreen Cladding

Cladding a building with timber boards is a wonderful way to finish a natural building and an excellent way to provide good weather protection that can last a very long time. It is important to ensure there is a good air gap behind the cladding and to ensure that any end grain in the timber boards is fully protected as that is where moisture can seep in and begin to rot the timber.

Timber boards can be of many different kinds and species providing they are laid either vertically or horizontally using the right detailing. Vertical boards need to overlap and be protected at the top by a good roof overhang. You can also lay boards side by side and cover the gap with a batten. Horizontal timber boards are best laid at an angle with a good overlap. You can source leftover waney edge boards for cladding as well as using ordinary timber. (51) If the wood is stained with good-quality oil-based timber stain (*see* Chapter 8) it can last for many years. Architects prefer to use vinegar-treated timber as they think it will be more robust. Others use cedar cladding with tongue and groove joints, although this may allow water to seep in.

There are also plastic cladding materials made to look like timber by combining polyethylene and wood fibres. (52)

Timber shingles on modernist house in Cambridge. (Photo: Mole Architects)

Timber boarding on Walter Segal frame houses at Allerton Park, Leeds, allowed to grey down naturally. (Photo: Jonathan Lindh)

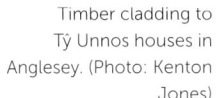

Timber cladding to Tŷ Unnos houses in Anglesey. (Photo: Kenton Jones)

Recycled Timber

It is possible to source second-hand timber. Demolition and salvage yards will have a range of timber taken out of buildings but it may not be possible to ascertain whether it was chemically treated or not. Creosote was often used on timber in the past as well as arsenic, and while these have since been banned they may remain on old timber. There are joinery workshops that are willing to work with recycled timber and you can get doors and window frames made out of wood such as pitch pine. Not all machinists like this as there can be old nails in the wood that can wreck saws. The advantage is that the quality of old wood is much higher than quicker-grown modern timber.

If you are lucky enough to have a recycling yard in your vicinity then it is sometimes possible to source recycled timber. Old railway sleepers still seem to be available and are often used in gardens, and there are companies that specialize in salvaged materials which come from (sadly) demolished old barns and other buildings. If you are renovating an old building it is ideal to find old salvaged materials that can match in with what has been retained. Old timber can have great character but also will have been from better

Timber buildings assembled from recycled wood and buildings at Holywood Men's Shed, Northern Ireland.

Woodland cabin built by Heimir Salt in Yorkshire. (Photo: Daniel Salt)

Recycled timber boards cladding woodland cabin.

wood than is usually available today. There are many companies exploiting this market and they know how to charge. Salvo is a directory of salvage yards and companies. (53) (54)

In Northern Ireland, where the author is based, many people have little interest or affection for older buildings and so there is extensive availability of recycled materials due to the over-demolition of perfectly sound buildings: over twenty-five salvage yards were identified in a quick internet search, though only two or three are members of Salvo.

Windows, Doors, Latches and Handles

Timber is the perfect material for doors and window frames. Builders seem determined to use uPVC windows and fibreglass doors wherever possible and many architects seem convinced that wooden windows will rot and want to use powder-coated aluminium, but for a natural finish and great quality timber is best. There are a range of composite timber internal doors which are widely used by housing developers because of their cheapness. Compressed from relatively poor-quality wood and moulded and painted, these doors can often look like they are made of plastic, which is apparently what the mainstream market desires. There are more expensive moulded doors, however, with wooden veneers and laminates in a wide range of styles. Builders' merchants and specialist door suppliers offer a wide range of solid wood doors, though much of the wood used is imported.

High-performance double- and triple-glazed timber windows are widely available, both imported and manufactured in the UK. There are timber windows with aluminium on the outside but the wood exposed on the inside. The British Woodworking Federation is a very useful source of information about doors and manufacturers in the UK as well as providing expertise and guidance on fire safety. (55) With over 500 members, the BWF sets high standards and provides a wealth of useful information on its website.

Locally made double-glazed timber frame window made from recycled pitch pine.

It's possible to find a range of wood door handles and latches which will complement the natural character of your building and these can be sourced in the UK. (56)

Low-Impact Uses of Wood

Many eco builders have tried to use the cordwood method in their buildings: this involves laying short log-like sections of timber set in a mortar bed of lime or clay. It is claimed that there are cordwood buildings in the US and Finland over 100 years old, but by and large this is not a very robust form of construction as it is very susceptible to rot. It attracts some self-builders as it looks easy to do but it does not provide a very thermally efficient form of walling. Unless extremely good well-seasoned wood is used the logs can shrink and split, leaving gaps in the wall which must be constantly repointed. However, some people find the cordwood look very attractive and often incorporate bottles as well, and there may be ways of incorporating cordwood into more energy-efficient solutions. (57) (58)

Saplings cut on site can be used to create a roof structure though this may not necessarily meet building regulations requirements!

Cordwood wall. (Photo: moduLog Celwood)

Roundwood poles used for roof structure. (Photo: Will Stanwix)

Walter Segal and the Segal Frame Method

Post and beam timber frame construction has been developed by a number of groups following a method pioneered by architect Walter Segal in the 1970s. The Segal method was a pioneering ecological approach as it was designed to minimize wastage of material and to touch the earth lightly through minimal foundations: the system made it easy to change the building and re-use, dismantle and recycle materials. There are many Segal frame housing projects throughout the UK and after a quiet period there has been a revival of interest. A timely new book by Grahame and McKean is a useful introduction

Three Walter Segal frame houses, Allerton Park, Leeds. (Photo: Jonathan Lindh)

to Segal's life and work and the impact of the Segal method. It is not a technical guide to the construction details but it does provide plenty of useful references and further reading. (59)

References

1. https://www.molearchitects.co.uk/eco-living/
2. https://www.parliament.uk/globalassets/documents/documents/upload/wtd10.pdf
3. https://newforestsawmill.co.uk/
4. http://www.forest-products.co.uk/
5. https://woodknowledge.wales/home-grown-homes
6. Ivor Davies, *Sustainable Construction Timber: Sourcing and Specifying Local Timber* (Forestry Commission, 2016).
7. https://fsc.org/en
8. https://www.pefc.org/
9. https://www.structuraltimber.co.uk/assets/InformationCentre/eb7.pdf
10. https://www.cbre.co.uk/services/business-lines/building-consultancy/build-insight/articles/the-future-of-engineered-timber-after-grenfell
11. https://www.trada.co.uk/news/what-is-the-future-for-timber-cladding-following-grenfell/
12. https://www.popularmechanics.com/home/outdoor-projects/a36166521
13. https://www.draxbiomass.com/
14. https://bylinetimes.com/2020/10/01/uk-drax-power-station-pillages-californian-forests/
15. Sam McBride, *Burned: The Inside Story of the Cash for Ash Scandal and Northern Ireland's Secretive New Elite* (Merrion Press, 2019).
16. https://www.letsrecycle.com/news/latest-news/veolia-reveals-extent-of-waste-wood-sent-to-landfill/
17. Almuth Ernsting, 'Burning Wood is Not the Answer', *The Land* (Issue 29, 2021).
18. https://www.smallwoods.org.uk/
19. http://www.donegalwoodlandowners.com/

20. Tony Wrench, *A Simple Roundhouse Manual* (Permanent Publications, 2015).
21. https://www.gilmouraitken.com/
22. https://www.woodproducts.fi/content/finnish-forests-3
23. https://www.thewpa.org.uk/wood-protection-treatments
24. https://www.accoya.com/uk/acetylation-what-is-it-and-what-is-acetylated-wood/
25. https://carpenteroak.com/expertise/encapsulation-systems/
26. https://www.borderoak.com/
27. https://www.oakwrights.co.uk/about/our-story/
28. https://www.oakmasters.co.uk/products/oak-framed-houses/
29. https://thecompleteoakhome.co.uk/
30. http://www.westwindoak.com/
31. https://www.primeoak.co.uk/
32. https://www.juliusbahn.co.uk/
33. https://www.welshoakframe.com/how-much-does-an-oak-frame-house-cost/
34. https://wyeoak.co.uk/
35. http://www.cabinliving.co.uk/logcabininsulation.asp#:~:text=Celotex%20or%20Kingspan%20insulation%20%2D%20ideal,at%20least%20this%20wall%20thickness
36. https://www.eco-home.ie/how-to-insulate-a-log-cabin/
37. https://www.britishlogcabins.com/log-homes
38. https://www.building.co.uk/news/persimmon-carrying-out-thousands-of-inspections-at-timber-frame-homes/5103681.article
39. https://www.mitek.co.uk/products/posi-joists/
40. https://opensourcewood.com/Pages/default.aspx
41. https://www.homebuilding.co.uk/advice/cross-laminated-timber
42. https://www.thinkwood.com/mass-timber/clt
43. https://www.napier.ac.uk/research-and-innovation/research-search/outputs/understanding-the-compatibility-of-uk-resource-for-dowel-laminated-timber-construction-1
44. https://www.building.co.uk/news/landg-ditches-structural-timber-in-modular-flats/5103249.article
45. http://www.eurban.co.uk/
46. https://www.binderholz.com/en-us/products/clt-bbs/
47. https://www.storaenso.com/en
48. https://www.tyunnos.co.uk/manufacture/
49. https://holzschindeln.com/
50. https://www.allgoodinthewood.co.uk/milled-sweet-chestnut-shingles/
51. https://www.vastern.co.uk/cladding/waney-edge-cladding/
52. https://ecoscapeuk.co.uk/blog/the-many-uses-of-wood-cladding/
53. https://www.englishsalvage.co.uk/beams-and-timber_itemcat_2012
54. https://www.salvoweb.com/salvo-directory/category/salvage-recycled-materials/location/uk/region/all
55. https://www.bwf.org.uk/
56. https://www.britishhardwoods.co.uk/oak-doors/solid-oak-door-fittings.html
57. https://accidentalhippies.com/2018/06/23/cordwood-beginners-faq/o
58. https://cordwoodconstruction.org/cordwood-mistakes
59. Alice Grahame and John McKean, *Walter Segal: Self-Built Architect* (Lund Humphries, 2021).

Chapter Four

LIME AND MASONRY

Lime and Cement

Using lime is an essential part of natural building. While some forms of earth and timber building may not require lime, strawbale building, hempcrete and any other forms of construction that require renders and plasters are usually dependent on lime to ensure healthy, breathable and weather-resistant construction. Lime has to be quarried and burned, emitting some CO_2, but has a lower embodied energy than cement and, as it dries, it carbonates, absorbing CO_2. Lime is softer and gentler than cement and it allows buildings to breathe and also provides a natural biocidal protection of timber and other materials.

Even though lime has to be manufactured in a kiln, it is viewed in this book as a natural material as, even after processing, lime remains closer to its natural state in the ground and can be returned to the ground after use without significant damage to the environment, unlike other chemicals like borax. Cement remains a toxic substance which can cause pollution.

The mixture of cement and sand, plus aggregates to make concrete, is one of the main materials of choice for the construction industry. Despite the fact that the production of cement is one of the biggest contributors to global warming, the UK alone consumes over 15 million tonnes every year. The cement industry has tried to reduce emissions through more efficient production processes and using waste material like power station ash, but so-called low-carbon cements bring with them new problems, possibly introducing a range of toxic chemicals and metals into buildings. Builders find cement mortars and renders easier to use and avoid lime which they regard as more difficult. However, chemicals are added to cement mixes to make them more workable and quicker to cure.

Many proprietary concrete screeds have chemicals added to induce quicker drying, which then give off gas into the buildings. Cement renders increasingly use polymer (plastic) additives and require plastic meshes to cope with movement that might cause cracking. You can escape many of these problems by using lime!

Using Lime

It is important for the natural builder to become familiar with the different forms of lime and how to use it, as it is not the same as mixing conventional cement and sand in a cement mixer. There are many organizations providing courses and training and so you can become proficient about using the material as a self-builder. Getting many mainstream builders and plasterers to use lime can prove to be difficult as they prefer to use cement and have a hundred and one excuses why, as well as charging over the odds for lime work.

If you are renovating or restoring an old building then lime may well be essential as many wonderful buildings have been ruined by the careless use of cement in the past. Conservation officers will be looking for you to use lime for pointing, rendering and plastering so that the old fabric of the building is not damaged. Even where a building is not historic or listed, such as a simple nineteenth-century brick terraced house, the original brickwork will have been done with lime mortars, though these may have been badly repaired with cement, allowing damp to enter. Lime versus cement has to be one of the most important battles in the world of sustainable building. In many developed countries, traditional and vernacular buildings that depended on lime mortar and plasters for their survival and comfort for the occupants have been devastated by ignorant builders (and even architects and surveyors) covering them with cement and concrete. There are many stories of people buying old (and not so old) buildings who have received a mortgage lending report warning of damp and what are sometimes called 'porous walls', with the requirement to install chemical damp-proof courses and cement renders to keep out the rain and 'rising damp'. Even worse is the advice to install internal insulated dry lining and to seal up the building to make it airtight to meet zero-carbon objectives. It can be quite difficult to avoid this if you are dependent on mortgage lending.

There are a wide range of views about the different forms of lime for different construction challenges: get three lime experts in a room and you may have five different opinions! As in the rest of the book, the attempt here is to provide neutral information about the range of possibilities as far as possible, and not get in the way of flying buckets of lime by taking sides.

There is no doubt that there are 'purists' in the lime world and they have very strong views about certain materials that they like and those they hate. Some experts have remarkable skills in analysing old lime in historic buildings and restoring cornices and pointing as authentically as possible. The self-builder on a tight budget may just be looking for a simple bag of the right kind of lime that they can get in their local merchants or a pre-formulated binder for hempcrete as they don't have time to become lime experts! It is worth looking briefly at the recent history of hydraulic lime to get a sense of some of the issues.

Natural Hydraulic Lime (NHL)

The Romans discovered hydraulic lime when they found that naturally occurring chalk and lime deposits, when contaminated with volcanic material, created a much stronger mortar for buildings which was also waterproof. This is generally associated with an area of Italy called Pozzuoli and you will come across references to pozzolans as additives to lime. Many ancient buildings are proof of this discovery. Some builders in countries like France continued to use lime in buildings and found large deposits of natural hydraulic lime (NHL), some underground, and lime is widely produced and used throughout Europe. Most hydraulic lime used in the UK today comes from France, Portugal and Italy as there were thought to be few, if any, deposits in the UK and Ireland. NHL could be mined in the UK and Ireland but such is the overbearing control of quarrying by a handful of multinational cement and aggregate companies that they have been able restrict access to natural lime deposits and the residents and planners in rural areas have opposed the extension of existing lime quarries.

It is not proposed to provide details of how lime is processed here as there are many better accounts such as the classic book by Holmes and Wingate. (1) It is important to understand what is known as the lime cycle, which describes the process by which lime is extracted from the ground, burned, mixed with water and eventually returns to its original state. This was well understood long before talk of the circular economy became fashionable.

It is possible to buy NHL in bags from a wide range of suppliers, some better than others. There

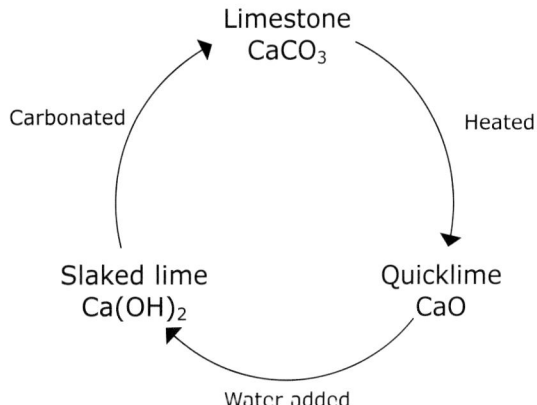

Diagram of the lime cycle. (Drawing: Lisa Ponzoni)

are three common grades of NHL: 2, 3.5 and 5. NHL 2 is described as feeble, 3.5 as moderate and 5 as eminently hydraulic. NHL 2 is best for internal plasters and soft masonry, moderate NHL for bedding and pointing and 5 is normally recommended for limecrete floors and exposed areas. This is where it begins to get difficult as some NHL 5 limes are so strong that they seem similar to cement. (2)

The classification of 2, 3.5 and 5 relates to the compressive strength of the lime and there are various relevant standards that define these. There is no doubt that this was influenced by the cement companies but fortunately some of the hydraulic lime producers are still reasonably independent. A very feeble lime classified as NHL 1 is also available.

The availability and ease of use of NHL products has definitely facilitated the greater use of lime instead of cement. However, it is not always the best form of lime to use for some building applications and many lime experts are concerned about the inappropriate use of NHL as it can be bought from mainstream merchants.

Hydrated or Air Limes

Air limes are non-hydraulic and are sometimes referred to as 'pure lime'. Calcium carbonate (limestone) from the ground is heated in a kiln to produce 'quicklime'. When it is mixed with water (slaking) it forms calcium hydroxide or hydrated or air lime. Hydrated lime can be ground into a powder (available in bags) or it can be kept as a thick paste known as lime putty or, when more liquid, as milk of lime. Powdered hydrated lime is often mixed with cement in what builders call 'gauging', which can make the cement mortar more elastic. This is sometimes presented by builders as lime render when in fact they are using a majority of cement. Hydrated limes can vary significantly in quality and you are best avoiding the bagged hydrated lime in many builders' merchants by obtaining good-quality air limes from lime specialist suppliers. Hydrated and hydraulic limes are sometimes blended to create lime binders, for hempcrete for instance.

Hot Limes

Some lime experts and masons are mistrustful of NHL limes and advocate greater use of hot-mix limes. Essentially hot-mix lime involves using quicklime: this is mixed with an aggregate (such as sand) and water is added to create a mortar, a process which then generates heat. Hot limes are weaker but preferred by masons who may add pozzolans. It is claimed that hot lime mortars are more breathable (vapour-permeable)

Tub of quicklime with sharp sand. (Photo: Nigel Copsey)

Water added to the quicklime. (Photo: Nigel Copsey)

Sand heaped over the lime to retain heat and left to 'cook'. (Photo: Nigel Copsey)

Resulting hot lime mortar after water added on completing of the slaking process. (Photo: Nigel Copsey)

and more durable. Hot lime pundits do not like NHLs, which they think are too hard and only suitable for underground work! (3) Nigel Copsey argues in his

very useful book for the revival of the use of what he calls traditional mortars. (4)

Applications of Lime

Rather than worrying about the different kinds of lime it is better to understand how different materials are suited to different applications. Patrick McAfee has written an excellent book that takes this approach; it is beautifully illustrated and shows the many different applications of lime. (5) McAfee discusses the traditional way in which quicklime was taken to site by horse and cart if kilns were not constructed on site. Ireland is particularly rich in chalk and limestone so old lime kilns still pepper the landscape. The quicklime could burst into flames if it got wet so great care had to be taken when transporting it. It was then made into lime putty or a hot lime mortar. He also explains how the ash created in lime burning could be added to lime to create a pozzolanic set much like NHL. Fine brick dust was also used. McAfee warns of the dangers of ignorant use of high-strength NHLs when repairing older buildings and his book is very useful as it sets out to answer many questions that home owners have put to him over the years.

Pointing of Stone and Brick Masonry

Pointing involves raking out the old joints, washing out and brushing, dampening, applying the mortar, 'pinning insertion' and 'galletting' (adding small stones), beating and finishing and then protecting the finished work to allow it to cure. There are hundreds of styles of pointing depending on the kind of stone and brick designs, from old rubble walls to new-build stone facing. There are many ways of finishing pointing with the pointing recessed, weather-struck, projecting and many more, the choice depending on aesthetics to some extent but also on which is best for the stone, brick and joints.

Old stone walls can be of many different hardnesses of stone and require the correct lime mortar for pointing and repair. (Photo: Lime Green)

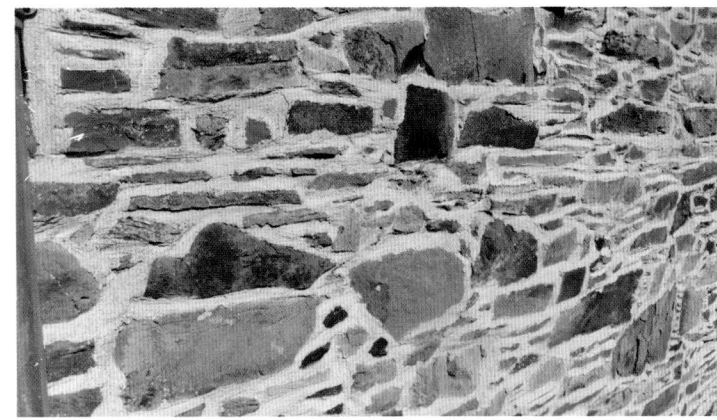

Rubble stone wall pointing with lime putty: after twenty-five years it looks as good as new.

Plastering onto Masonry Walls

Traditional plaster was made with lime putty. The older the putty the better and it was often left in a pit for months. Hydrated lime can be rehydrated to create a putty. Lime putty plaster can be applied to wooden lathes. Plastering onto masonry involves lime mixed with sand. Sometimes horsehair is used and usually three layers are built up with none more than 12mm thick. Lime putty can also be gauged with plaster of Paris and mixed with the sand. Lime plasters can be sprayed using suitable machinery.

External Renders

External lime renders are called 'wet dash' in Ireland, 'harling' in Scotland and 'roughcast' in England. Various kinds of lime can be used with sand, including NHL, high calcium and so on. The size of the sand aggregate depends on what appearance is required: smooth or very rough. Normally, sharp sand is used. Lime renders can be used on modern masonry construction, hempcrete and strawbale walls and sometimes applied to cob and earth walls.

The natural builder should avoid the use of cement renders as this can cause enormous damage to natural

Initial coat of lime plaster on masonry wall. (Photo: Lime Green)

Lime-spraying machine. (Photo: Lime Green)

buildings by trapping moisture. Different mixes can be used though normally a lime render will use three parts of sharp sand to one of lime. If you intend to do your own rendering and plastering but have little experience then it's essential to go on a course to learn how to do it well.

An innovative ready-mixed lime plaster which can be used externally or internally is called Limecote. It is a non-hydraulic lime plaster which comes dry and ready to be mixed with water. A synthetic reinforcing fibre (in tiny quantities) is mixed in to strengthen the render against cracking. It does not contain sand or any other aggregates. The manufacturers claim that Limecote is based on a medieval recipe for lime plaster and it has the advantage of being very flexible and able to cope with movement in timber structures, whereas other heavier renders can crack. It is made from chalk from East Anglia and Derbyshire lime. (6)

Its manufacturers also make a product called Warmcote which they say is an insulating lime plaster with good thermal performance but as it is a fairly new product it was not possible to find any independent evaluation of this. However, Warmcote

External lime render completed in major refurbishment of the nine-bedroom House of the Northern Gate on Dunnet Head, the most northerly part of mainland UK: the house is fully exposed to severe weather. (Photo: Lime Green)

and Limecote can be applied to a very wide range of materials and if you are nervous about doing lime plastering as a self-builder, it's worth looking at this material as it is claimed to be easy to use.

Limewashing

Lime-rendered and masonry buildings were traditionally limewashed. Over the years this has been replaced by acrylic (plastic) masonry paints, which are assumed to be much better. Plastic paints will deteriorate over time. Limewashing, however, may have been done every year even though this is not essential. Limewashing inside agricultural buildings like cattle byres was normal because the lime acts as an antiseptic. Limewashing also helped to reinforce lime renders. Weak mixes of lime putty and water are best for limewashing, with several coats applied. Various pigments can be included to give coloured finishes and tallow or linseed oil added to improve water resistance, though this can reduce the breathability. Breathable mineral silicate paints are available today to use on lime renders but it is still worth considering using the old limewash.

Buildings used for food processing such as cheese making are required by environmental health agencies to cover all surfaces with uPVC and stainless steel even though these need to be cleaned frequently with toxic cleaning materials. You are unlikely to get a positive response if you suggest going back to the old-fashioned antiseptic limewash!

When to Use Cement

Despite the damage to the planet caused by cement there are some situations in which using cement for its greater strength may be necessary. Concrete foundations are common, but there are ways of minimizing these by using point loading onto small pads or even tyres.

Limecrete can be used to replace concrete floors and screeds. Concrete blocks are cheap and easily obtainable and may be essential if you are building below ground level but the general rule should be to minimize cement and concrete as much as possible.

Limecrete Floors

Limecrete floors are a breathable alternative to concrete and cement screed floors. However, if there are high radon levels at your site then an impermeable radon barrier will have to be used and this will prevent the floor from being breathable. Where radon is not a problem then insulation from materials like foamed glass can be used with a geotextile layer topped with NHL and sand screed. The floor can then be tiled with a lime mortar bedding. A range of lime specialist suppliers can provide advice and technical information.

Renovating Old Brick and Stone Walls

Older buildings may have been repainted with cement mortar in the mistaken belief that this will reduce rain penetration. This can even lead to deterioration of the brickwork. Walls may have been rendered with cement or pebble-dash and this can sometimes be difficult to remove without damaging the old masonry beneath. Old stone and brick walls can be repointed with lime mortar and lime renders can be applied if the masonry is not to be left exposed, particularly where there may be driving rain. The *Old House Eco Handbook* by Suhr and Hunt provides a very useful guide to wall types. (7)

Dampness and Damp-Proof Courses

When buying an older property, it is not unusual to come across problems of dampness and if you require a mortgage you will invariably be asked by the bank or building society to install a damp-proof course (DPC). For good measure there may also be an instruction to spray the roof with toxic chemicals to protect against woodworm. While there may well be problems with damp and occasional problems with woodworm or dry rot, the standard solutions requested by building societies are often costly and not always appropriate. Indeed, they may have already been done a few years before but the previous guarantee may be lost or not accepted as many companies doing this work go out of business. Very often the chemical damp-proof courses injected into walls can do more harm than good and may not deal with the damp problem at all.

The cause of damp may well be due to broken downpipes, earth piled up against a wall bridging the old DPC, blocked drains or the absence of adequate drainage around the foot of the existing walls. Mortgage surveyors could easily identify these problems rather than taking the lazy course of advocating a new DPC to be carried out by a local company that they are probably very friendly with! An organization called Heritage House has been campaigning for many years about this problem and says that the Royal Institute of Chartered Surveyors has recently recognized there is a problem. Increasingly, householders worry about chemical treatment in their homes and will search for more natural solutions. Natural solutions can include simple maintenance but also the replacement of cement renders with breathable materials. (8) DPCs are necessary in some forms of construction but injected silicone and other methods can make damp worse rather than better.

Building New Walls with Stone and Brick

In Chapter 2, the problem of fake brick slip walls on timber frame construction was discussed. It is less common today for houses to be constructed with conventional brick cavity walls and it is hard to say whether this is a sustainable solution for the future. Generally, today's brick walls are constructed with cement mortars which means they cannot be recycled other than as crushed rubble. Stone facing is also becoming very popular as a range of thin slate and stone-effect tiles are sold as facing for buildings. These products, sometimes referred to as stone veneers or stone wall effect panels, are generally glued onto to back boards or concrete block walls with polymer cement adhesives. While this might give a natural look to a building it is not a very natural solution.

If you can manage to source second-hand bricks or stones then these can provide a useful addition to a natural building if lime mortars are used. Brick and stone plinths for cob, strawbale and hempcrete walls can be used as well as rainscreen cladding but this can be expensive and time-consuming. Celtic Sustainables advertise that they have salvaged stone.

Sourcing Lime, Getting Advice and Training

There are many places where you can obtain some lime in bags such as NHL and hydrated lime but if you want to use the right materials it is best to go to a specialist lime supplier, who may also be able to provide good advice and possibly offer training courses and workshops.

The UK and Irish Building Limes Forums provide extensive information and education about limes. Their websites include lists of suppliers, though this is by no means complete, with some surprising omissions, and there may be more in your locality. Below is a list of a few examples but there are many more and it is worthwhile finding out about lime as it's an essential component of natural building.

Selected Lime Suppliers and Information Sources

Cornish Lime Company, Cornwall (9)

Heritage Ltd, Northern Ireland (10)

Masons Mortar, Edinburgh (11)

Tŷ-Mawr Lime Ltd, Powys, Wales (12)

Mike Wye & Associates, Devon (13)

Celtic Sustainables, Ceredigion, Wales (14)

Lime Green Products Ltd, Shropshire (15)

Earth, Stone & Lime Company, Yorkshire (16)

Building Limes Forum UK, Edinburgh (lists numerous centres) (17)

Anglia Lime Company, Suffolk (18)

Scottish Lime Centre, Fifeshire (19)

West Dean College, Chichester, West Sussex (20)

The Lime Centre, Winchester, Hampshire (21)

Society for the Protection of Ancient Buildings, London (22)

References

1. Stafford Holmes and Michael Wingate, *Building with Lime: A Practical Introduction* (Practical Action, 1999).
2. https://www.lime-mortars.co.uk/lime-mortar/hydraulic
3. https://www.hotmixedmortars.com/
4. Nigel Copsey, *Hot Mixed Lime and Traditional Mortars: A Practical Guide to Their Use in Conservation and Repair* (The Crowood Press, 2019).
5. Patrick McAfee, *Lime Works: Using Lime in Traditional and New Buildings* (Associated Editions, 2009).
6. https://bestoflime.co.uk/product/limecote/
7. Marianne Suhr and Roger Hunt, *Old House Eco Handbook* (Frances Lincoln, 2019).
8. https://www.heritage-house.org/damp-and-condensation/rics-joint-dampness-methodology-statement.html
9. www.cornishlime.co.uk
10. www.heritageltd.com
11. www.masonsmortar.co.uk
12. www.lime.org.uk
13. www.mikewye.co.uk
14. www.celticsustainables.co.uk
15. https://www.lime-green.co.uk/info/trade
16. http://www.nigelcopsey.com/
17. https://www.buildinglimesforum.org.uk/about-lime/courses-on-lime/
18. http://www.anglialime.com/
19. www.scotlime.org
20. www.westdean.org.uk/BCM
21. www.thelimecentre.co.uk
22. www.spab.org.uk

Chapter Five

STRAWBALE BUILDING

Why Use Straw for Building?

After earth, straw is a frequently used material for construction around the world by natural builders, but strawbale construction is less common in the UK and Ireland than it is elsewhere in Europe.

Strawbale (SB) construction developed in the US in the 1970s and is referred to as the strawbale revival because early pioneers in the nineteenth century constructed houses out of straw, particularly when no other materials were readily available. Load-bearing SB houses are often referred to as Nebraska-style because SB buildings, now over 100 years old, were constructed on the great plains of America, such as the Burke house in Bayard, Nebraska, built in 1903. (1) Many of the pioneering books and guides about SB originate in the US and standards and certification have been achieved so that SB buildings can comply with American building codes. (2)

Straw is more commonly used in developing countries, mixed with earth to make cob or adobe, whereas bale construction relies on the availability of baling machines to create the familiar rectangular bales. Increasingly, with the industrialization of agriculture, straw is baled in huge round or rectangular bales largely unsuitable for building. In some cases, SB builders have tried to remake bales using old baling machines but this is not easy to achieve. As will be seen, straw can also be used compacted into prefabricated panels.

Many people confuse straw bales with hay bales, but hay is generally unsuitable for construction as it is mostly leafy material. A hay building might get eaten by a passing donkey as hay is a food source. Straw is the leftover stem material from the production of crops such as oat, wheat, barley, rice, maize and so on. When the plant has been harvested and processed into flour and seeds, then straw is left on the ground or burnt off. It is used for animal bedding and in mushroom farms where it is rotted down with manure.

SB construction is widely seen as one of the most ecological, low-impact ways to build as it is using a natural bio-based 'waste' material that can provide

Self-built timber frame and strawbale house on Exmoor in Devon. (Photo: Justin Tyers)

a healthy, breathable, well-insulated structure. SB attracts self-build eco enthusiasts who assume that straw is cheap and that SB buildings will therefore be cheap. However, straw can be in great demand and is not always cheap and plentiful if crops have failed. Strawbale buildings can be complicated and difficult to build and great care needs to be taken to use the correct construction techniques and to build properly with SB, so it is not necessarily cheap. There are some SB buildings in the UK, but many more in Europe, and by and large they are the work of enthusiastic self-builders rather than being found in mainstream construction. Commercial house builders are unlikely to use SB but there are a few examples of large 'public' buildings using straw included here.

SB enthusiasts can be passionate and will protest at any comments about difficulty and cost, but it is better to be sensible and realistic if embarking on an SB building. Excellent moisture control is critical in strawbale buildings, as plasters can leak and straw will rot if it gets damp. It is essential to attend a strawbale training course or work with companies that specialize in SB, particularly for load-bearing structures or when infilling a timber frame with straw-bales. However, some self-builders have built buildings by infilling straw bales within timber frames without getting specialist help. If you are considering embarking on a strawbale project it would be a good idea to obtain a recent book by Nitzkin and Termans, A *Complete Guide to Straw Bale Building*, (3) which is an indispensable 300-page guide: this chapter will only give a summary of the different aspects of SB; Nitzkin and Termans go into much more detail.

One reason for the lack of SB buildings in UK and Ireland is that there have been some strawbale failures constructed in a careless way, unlike the many excellent projects illustrated in Nitzkin and Termans' book (though the book includes very few UK examples). While SB buildings can resist the weather, and make excellent buildings, they need to be designed, constructed and finished carefully and their guide provides a lot of useful technical advice.

A further problem has been the failure of the very small SB community in the UK to set about obtaining certification and establishing standards as has been done in the US, France and Germany, and until this is done, SB is unlikely to play a big part in low-carbon construction in the UK and Ireland. However, there has been a significant change in the last few years, with a revival of interest in SB with many young people setting up new organizations to promote the use of straw, including Straw-Bale Building UK (SBUK), and this has already led to more projects appearing.

A European project, UPSTRAW, (4) has catalogued the many SB projects around Europe and has recently published a 2020 yearbook which emphasizes the use of straw in larger public buildings.

The Science, Design and Structural Aspects of SB

Straw bales can be used in several different ways to create insulated walls and even floors and roofs. Use in roofs and floors is less common but careful design and detailing can avoid possible problems if the bales do not get wet. In walls, straw bales can be load-bearing, which is a particular advantage of the material, but they can also be used in various infill frames and hybrid arrangements. Loose straw is also being increasingly used, compressed into timber frame prefabricated panels.

When straw is baled the strands of straw are laid in a particular direction and this gives added strength to the bales. If the bales are laid on their edge, some of the structural strength is lost but this can still work. The bales are held together with baler twine and this is an important part of the structure. If bales are to be cut then the new smaller bales must be tied tightly with twine to maintain the original compression.

In wall construction, it is normal practice to reinforce and tie the bales together. One form of reinforcement is to drive hazel rods through the bales but this is not essential as bales can also be tied on the outside and bale walls can be strapped tightly together and tied to a roof plate and floor plate. The bottom row of bales can be staked onto wooden or metal spikes. There are various different techniques for compressing the bales into place within a wall system, and each has its advocates. While most of these processes are quite simple it can be seen that training and experience in how to put bales together is important and may not fully be understood from books and drawings.

A load-bearing wall (often referred to as Nebraska-style) requires a wall plate and floor plate/ foundation. When a heavy load such as a roof is supported by such a wall the bales will compress, so allowance has to be made for this. If straw bales are used as infill in, say, a timber frame structure the bales may still reduce in size a little: gaps at the tops of walls should be spotted and eliminated. Nitzkin and Ternans' book shows a whole range of options for wall systems and even shows jacks or straps used to compress bales as the wall is raised.

Load-Bearing Bale Walls

It is possible to build two-storey load-bearing SB buildings. Denser straw bales are advised for strength, but most Nebraska-style buildings are single-storey. The bales are laid in a staggered bond and should not normally exceed seven rows; they should not be more than six metres in length without some kind of cross-bracing. Crucial to load-bearing construction are wall plates and compression. A considerable amount of scientific work has been done on the load-bearing capacity of SB and its performance under seismic loads based on testing. Details can be found in Appendix A of the Nitzkin and Termans book (and in New Zealand Earth Building Standard 4299).

Wall top plates are a crucial element of load-bearing construction. These can be constructed in various ways, such as a ladder frame or solid boards which are then strapped down to the footings of the

Strawbale extension building in Walderchain Wood, Kent, showing use of timber wall plate and rafters. (Photo: Mark Saich)

Walderchain strawbale building with load-bearing construction, showing the wall plate on top of the bales. (Photo: Mark Saich)

building. Depending on what form of reinforcement and strapping is used the wall plates can help to compress the straw.

Bale Infill Walls

Bales can be used as infill in many different forms of frame construction, such as post and beam, but the timber frame structure has to be designed to accommodate the width of the bales. The bales need to be reinforced in such a way that they are tied to the timber frame posts and floor and wall plates. Ideally the dimension of the section to be infilled should be sized so that the bales are tightly packed. In theory concrete and steel frame systems could also be infilled with bales but this is uncommon as it can lead to condensation problems where the bales meet the impervious materials. Using bales for infill with

timber frame is the easiest way to build with bales and is much simpler than load-bearing.

There are numerous options for the design of constructions, usually using timber posts or double studs that are then infilled with bales. Posts can be notched into the bales or in the middle of bales; double posts are frequently used or columns made from I-beams or boards. The timber structure can be closely spaced with one bale between each upright or further apart. There is an example of this in an Italian guide to natural building showing straw bales infilled with timber posts. (5)

Buildings can be constructed with some structural support from timber but also with compressed walls

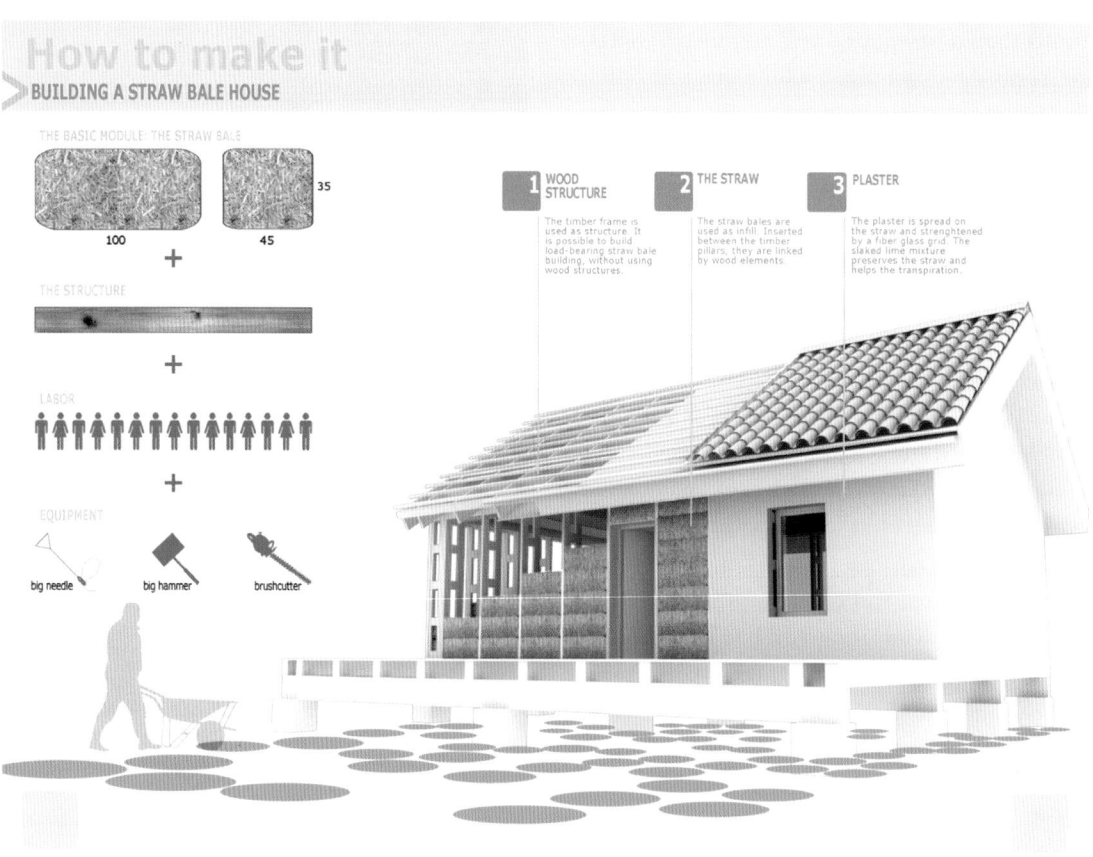

Method of using bales infilled between timber uprights. (Drawing: Casa di Paglia, Beyond Architecture Group, Italy)

and infills. There is a great deal of flexibility, which gives wider scope for a range of hybrid structures.

Prefabricated Panels

Normally, prefabricated straw panels are made from a timber box frame into which full bales are inserted or, more commonly, loose straw is packed. There are a range of options available and it is possible to create your own prefabricated panels though this may not acceptable under the building regulations. There are at least two commercially available prefabricated strawbale panel systems available, ModCell and EcoCocon. ModCell has been constructing prefabricated strawbale panel buildings for many years and recent projects include commercial housing and school buildings. It would not be possible to tell by looking at some of these projects that straw bales have been used, when the buildings are clad with more conventional materials such as fibre boards or brick.

Conventional SB construction normally uses an external lime-based render to maintain breathability and tends to have a strawbale look, but this need not be the case with prefabricated panels. It is not uncommon for the prefabricated panels to be covered with a plastic airtightness membrane in an effort to achieve very good thermal performance, and while such membranes are meant to be vapour-permeable, some may feel that this defeats the purpose of using a natural breathable material such as straw.

The advantage of using prefabricated panels is that they are engineered and made off site or on site in a 'flying factory' but ready to incorporate into a building, arriving on the back of a truck and usually craned into position. The advantage of prefabricated panels for hempcrete, for instance, is that the walls are able to dry out before arriving on site but this is less of an issue with strawbale unless the prefabrication also involves lime renders. This can simplify the construction process and mainstream builders are likely to be happier to incorporate an engineered panel product into their building.

EcoCocon

EcoCocon are based in Lithuania and state that they offer 'exact and precise panels with evenly compressed straw with rapid erection', though this may require the use of a crane. They offer a wide range of sizes of panels and the load-bearing timber frame used can apparently support three storeys. They say that their buildings can achieve a U value of $0.11\,W/m^2K$ and meet passivhaus standards. They have a range of technical approvals and performance declarations, with Class B flammability certification and Cradle to Cradle certification, but the fire rating will be based on cladding with other non-flammable materials.

While EcoCocon seem, as a general rule, to use breather membranes, they also use cladding such as wood fibre for airtightness and additional insulation. Their buildings also use lime renders. EcoCocon have UK agents for their system.

EcoCocon prefabricated panels with timber bracing (Photo: EcoCocon)

EcoCocon prefabricated panels being craned into position.
(Photo: EcoCocon)

ModCell

The ModCell system uses the thermal insulation qualities of straw and timber to form structural prefabricated panels. 'ModCell allows super-insulated, high-performance, low energy "passive" buildings to be built using renewable, locally sourced, carbon sequestering materials that include straw and wood to create a less than zero carbon construction system.' (6)

A list of some ModCell projects below shows how extensively this off-site technology has been used. ModCell also advertise that mortgages are available for their houses from the Ecology Building Society.

ModCell housing project, Rochester Road, Bristol; it is not at all obvious that these have been built with straw. (Photo: ModCell)

ModCell's Ysgol Rhyd y Llan School in Anglesey; it is not obvious that this is built with straw panels due to the use of external cladding. (Photo: ModCell)

ModCell used with internal timber lining in Yeotown retreat centre, Devon. (Photo: Guy Harrop)

LILAC Project

The LILAC project in Leeds is a well-known co-housing project. (7) Taking many years to get going, the scheme consists of twenty eco houses managed by residents through a mutual ownership society. It set out from the beginning to be a model of ecological, affordable living, with shared facilities, beautiful landscaping and vegetable gardens as well as eventually choosing to use the ModCell strawbale construction system. (8) LILAC participants claim they use 66 per cent less energy than conventional housing, though much of this is due to the photovoltaic panels they have on their roofs.

Having visited LILAC several times during construction, it was clear that there were some teething problems with the strawbale panels, and the design of the top of the walls and roof junction looked capable of causing problems, with staining on the walls where there were no overhangs. However, today the houses look well maintained and in very good condition. An early principle of using natural materials and lime renders was that houses should have 'a good hat and pair of boots', which implies the use of good roof overhangs. However, modern architecture with flat roofs and no overhangs has been very much in vogue and can present some detailing challenges when using natural materials. Even though there are flat-roof SB buildings without any roof overhangs, this is not generally to be recommended.

LILAC block (Leeds), showing flat roof design without overhangs.

LILAC strawbale panel walls under construction with some teething problems with internal render.

Other ModCell Projects

ModCell has been used to create some luxury holiday cottages as part of a health retreat in Yeotown in North Devon. The buildings feature a swaying meditation pod with a hemp rope, and a range of health and wellness treatments and courses are available. It is described as having a stylish rustic-chic décor but the strawbale construction does not feature on the website! (9)

ModCell strawbale panels have been used in a £4.5 million school in Llanfaethlu, Anglesey, in North Wales, for Anglesey County Council; the contractors were Wynne Construction. The project won a Construction Excellence award in 2018. It would not be obvious that the buildings include straw bales, as the external cladding is a product called Rockclad which is made from compressed basalt mineral wool fibres and thermo-hardening synthetic binders. The surface of the panels is treated with a polymer emulsion coating. (10)

Straw Bales in the Construction Process

Floors and Roofs

It is possible to use straw bales in both roof and floor construction. It is essential to create a structure which is deep enough and strong enough to

Straw bales used to insulate roof in the far north of Scotland. (Photo: Bernard Planterose, North Woods Design)

Straw bales used to insulate roof. (Photo: Bernard Planterose, North Woods Design)

to use bales in suspended floors and not buried in concrete floors, though this has been tried! Roof construction should always be well ventilated using breathable materials to avoid condensation. North Woods Construction are a timber frame and sawmill company in the north of Scotland and have used straw bales in the roof of their workshop building. (11)

Finishing Strawbale Walls

It is normal practice to render strawbale walls with lime and sand renders and plasters. This can provide an external weathering coat but it is vitally important that a breathable material based on lime is used. Clay renders and plasters may possibly also be used in more sheltered areas, behind a ventilated rain-screen cladding or internally. Early strawbale buildings used various forms of mesh tied to the bales to create a key for the renders but this is not necessary and an initial scratch coat can be created by pushing the render into the straw. This is a labour-intensive process and a quicker method would be to use a lime spraying kit.

External cladding such as a timber rainscreen can be used with SB walls. It is best practice to ensure that there is a ventilated gap between the SB and the cladding and the straw should be covered with a render which can remain rough as it will not be seen. Strawbale walls need to be fully encapsulated with materials impervious to water vapour to prevent the easy transfer of moist air into the walls, while allowing any moisture within the wall to escape.

Strawbale and Fires

It is normal for strawbale enthusiasts to minimize the issue of fire risk in strawbale construction. There are always warnings about not leaving

support the bales and to ensure that both are well ventilated to ensure that there is no danger of moisture or condensation build-up. It is only possible loose straw lying around on site as this has been the cause of many SB fires during construction. Nitzkin and Termans devote very little attention to the issue and the word 'fire' does not appear in the index. A literature search provided surprisingly few studies of fire resistance of strawbale construction. In theory, densely packed straw should provide little oxygen for a fire to develop but it is essential to have a continuous fireproof render. A reasonably thick lime or earth render is essential inside and out in order to provide fire protection for the strawbale walls. The straw cannot be left exposed unlike with hempcrete. Hemp lime renders have also been used with strawbale. In Australia and California, rendered strawbale walls have resisted bush fires, and tests that demonstrate very good fire resistance have been carried out in the US and Australia.

A conference paper from 2017 by Sanin Dzidic of the University of Bihać in Bosnia suggests that there is still need for more research on fire and SB construction: (12)

Reinforcing mesh round window opening. (Photo March Saich)

> Knowledge on fire resistance of elements made of straw bales is still incomplete and requires more fire resistance testing, that will take in consideration type of straw, its chemical composition, density of straw bales, composition and design of different kits made of straw bales including the other factors and even large-scale tests not conducted on building elements only …

Bath University has subjected a prefabricated strawbale panel house to a fire test and it survived for over two hours but this was done in 2009. (13) An interesting report of the effects of recent wildfires on strawbale buildings in California by David Arkin includes details of fire tests by the Ecological Building Network in the US. Four case studies claim that strawbale buildings had some damage due to wildfires but still performed better than conventional stick-framed buildings. (14)

Windows and Doors

The detailing around windows and doors requires careful attention in strawbale construction, especially to prevent ingress of external moisture, by using details that shed water to the exterior of the cladding. There are a variety of options for creating timber box or post frames in the walls. The frame needs to be built into the wall as the bales are raised. Reinforcing mesh is normally required to avoid cracking when the render is applied and meets the frame. Window sills are particularly

Tyre foundation ready to receive box beam. (Photo: Richard Stacy)

Box beam under construction. (Photo: Richard Stacy)

important to ensure that rain doesn't seep into the wall just below windows.

Foundations and Footings

It's not uncommon to find examples of strawbale buildings using recycled tyres as foundations. The argument in favour of this solution is that it reduces the use of cement and concrete which are normally used for foundations. Normally, a timber box frame sits on the car tyres and this has been accepted by

building control. There is a useful discussion available of this approach from the builder of a strawbale cottage in Suffolk. (15)

Examples of SB Houses in the UK

There are many examples of self-build SB houses in the UK, some being the homes of the builders but others let as holiday cottages. A few examples are discussed here. Some people are attracted by the natural qualities of straw but others were aiming to create very energy-efficient homes and even attempt to achieve the extreme energy-efficient passivhaus standard. A house in Norfolk built by Fran Bradshaw of Ann Thorne Architects may have just failed to achieve passivhaus certification initially but this may have been corrected subsequently. (16)

Another project, Haven Cottage in Stowmarket, Suffolk, was awarded passivhaus accreditation in 2015/16. Haven Cottage has been particularly well documented by the self-builders Dave and Mabel Howorth and their architect Andrew Goodman. The project has hosted open days and training workshops and a detailed description can be found in *Passive House Plus* magazine. (17)

While Haven Cottage is quite modern in design, its builders tried to emulate a Dutch barn and the

Haven Cottage, Suffolk, under construction. (Photo: Andrew Goodman Good Architecture)

Haven Cottage, rear elevation finished. (Photo: Agnese Sanvito)

Haven Cottage, front elevation. (Photo: Agnese Sanvito)

use of traditional lime render on the strawbale walls aimed to be sympathetic to the local vernacular. While the walls were made from straw bales, the floor used a polystyrene and concrete system, with recycled newspaper insulation in the aluminium-covered roof.

Sam Atkinson is a self-employed carpenter and has built several strawbale houses in Yorkshire and Cumbria, inspired by his mother's pioneering strawbale buildings which are now let as holiday cottages. (18) These projects demonstrate that strawbale construction can meet the needs of people who want simple affordable houses of different styles with different finishes, including timber rainscreen.

Justin and Linda Tyers have lived for a number of years on a sailing boat but decided to self-build a house on Exmoor National Park on a very limited budget. Using local timber from a nearby sawmill and strawbales from a local farmer, their house is off-grid, relying on photovoltaic (PV) panels for electricity. The site was bought for £50,000 under a National Park affordable housing scheme and they claim to have built the house for £67,000. Given the high quality of the finishes and interiors this might seem hard to believe but they did most of the building work themselves. (19) They are supporters of the Exmoor Young Voices organization which is trying to find ways of making it possible for young people to self-build affordable houses in the area. (20)

Strawbale house by Sam Atkinson in Yorkshire. (Photo: Sam Atkinson)

Strawbale house by Sam Atkinson in Cumbria. (Photo: Sam Atkinson)

Interior of Justin and Linda Tyers' Exmoor house. (Photo: Justin Tyers)

Jim Carfrae, a research fellow at Plymouth University, was an early pioneer of strawbale construction, building a large post and frame building with strawbale infill in Totnes in 2003–07. He has done a great deal of research on strawbale and other natural construction materials. Featured here is a house in Devon called 'Long View' which is a composite of straw bales and timber with sheep's wool insulation in the roof. The bales have a rough lime render for fireproofing and are then covered with a timber rainscreen. This house has won the South West Federation of Master Builders' regional award.

Strawbale walls under construction, 'Long View', Devon. (Photo: Jim Carfrae)

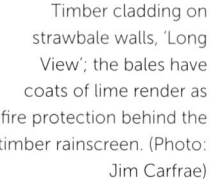

Timber cladding on strawbale walls, 'Long View'; the bales have coats of lime render as fire protection behind the timber rainscreen. (Photo: Jim Carfrae)

Richard and Rachel Stacy's strawbale holiday cottage in Suffolk before plastering; the ties from wall plate to floor can be clearly seen. (Photo: Richard Stacy)

Interior of Stacy Strawbale cottage. (Photo Richard Stacy)

Richard and Rachel Stacy built a strawbale cottage in Suffolk and have provided a wonderful documentation of the construction process about the problems and decisions they had to make. Located in Haughley Green near Bury St Edmunds, the cottage was self-built with the help of a few friends and is now let as a holiday cottage. Constructed on box beams built off re-used tyre foundations, they use threaded Acrow poles to winch the roof plate down onto the strawbale walls. The roof was added at an early stage to give protection to the walls; it is made from prefabricated steel and plastic foam insulated panels, a simple and easy solution, though not at all ecological! (21)

In a remote part of Moray in northern Scotland is a strawbale holiday house called 'Hobbit Hideaway',

'Hobbit Hideaway' holiday cottage in Moray, Scotland, external view. (Photo: A. White)

'Hobbit Hideaway', Moray, showing use of local wood in interior. (Photo: A. White)

which was built with the help of Hartwyn who provide training and courses on strawbale construction courses. It has won the Best Green Holiday Home award of the European Holiday Home Association. (22)

Lough Mardal Lodge is a holiday development in Donegal where the main accommodation is in off-grid yurts. However, the main facilities building has been constructed with roundwood timber with strawbale walls and a reciprocal roof with a very large span. (23)

Lough Mardal Lodge, interior, with strawbale walls plastered. (Photo: Marcus Tindal)

Lough Mardal Lodge, Donegal, interior, showing use of roundwood timber and strawbale walls under construction. (Photo: Marcus Tindal)

Community Buildings

One of the attractions of SB building is the opportunity for communities of people to join together to take part in ecological building. It's not surprising that this has attracted some church groups. One example is a tiny round strawbale building, Gwalia Chapel in north Wales, which was designed by Andy Hales and is also illustrated by John Butler Consultancy. (24) A much bigger project is a large church

West gable of Tulse Hill church hall, showing bale infill. (Photo: Richard Dormandy and Nicole Lyon)

Hammering a bale into position at Tulse Hill. (Photo: Richard Dormandy and Nicole Lyon)

Strawbale-infilled wall, Tulse Hill. (Photo: Richard Dormandy and Nicole Lyon)

Tulse Hill, south elevation showing PV panels on roof. (Photo: Richard Dormandy and Nicole Lyon)

community building in Tulse Hill in south London, Holy Trinity and St Matthias. This ambitious project was the vision of the vicar Richard Dormandy and the church community, not just for a new community hall, but a community building exercise in which participating in strawbale construction was central. Sadly, due to Covid the levels of group participation had to be cut back and at the time of writing the church is still raising funds to complete the building. However, as can be seen from the photographs this large and ambitious project is well advanced and demonstrates that scale should not be a limitation for straw bales. (25)

Hartwyn are a small company that combine design and build services with information and resources to provide assistance for people wanting to carry out natural building. They say they aim to create high-performance structures blending heritage techniques with new technologies. Hartwyn have done a number of strawbale buildings using innovative timber structures and run a range of training workshops.

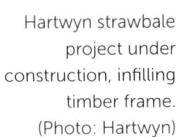

Hartwyn strawbale project under construction, infilling timber frame. (Photo: Hartwyn)

Hartwyn strawbale project, finished interior. (Photo: Hartwyn)

The National Trust have constructed a strawbale visitor centre building in Cumbria known as the Footprint Building. Its construction can be followed on a set of time-lapse photos. (26) The bales are infilled into a timber frame and finished with a lime render designed by Crosby Granger Architects of Kendal. (27) It is disappointing that the National Trust has not taken more of a lead on sustainable buildings and materials as their focus seems to be have been much more on 'green' energy. There have been other proposals to build with natural materials but these have run into planning problems. The National Trust HQ building in Swindon was an innovative project but without a focus on natural materials.

Strawbale Advice, Resources and Approvals

Given the absence of approved standards and certification for SB in the UK it might seem difficult to achieve approval for strawbale buildings under the building regulations. To date most strawbale buildings have received approval without too much difficulty, thanks to the current flexibility of UK regulations; however, this may become more difficult in the future following misplaced paranoia about fire safety following Grenfell. This should have led to greater restrictions on the use of flammable plastic foam materials, but instead there are proposals to limit the use of timber and natural materials. While it may be possible to navigate building regulations without too much difficulty, there seem to be growing problems with planning approval.

There are recent examples of SB buildings being refused planning permission on some occasions, most recently by Calderdale Council for a modest SB house in Hebden Bridge in West Yorkshire. (28) However, it is not necessarily the case that such projects are turned down because they are made from straw bales but for other planning reasons. Anyone making an application for planning permission is well advised *not* to refer to it as a strawbale house as the planning policies do not dictate what materials a house is made from, though they can have significant restrictions on the external appearance and this may mitigate against the proposed use of natural materials.

The application for the Hebden Bridge SB project shows the applicant went to considerable trouble to put forward a well-argued proposal for an off-grid, low-impact natural building, but the site was unfortunately just in the green belt and local councillors used this as the reason for refusal. No doubt an adept planning consultant might have found a way round this but unfortunately current planning policies do not provide any additional points for sustainable low-impact projects.

Lilly's Cottage, near Axminster, drawing of interior combining cob and strawbale. (Drawing: Rachel Collins)

Another proposal for a strawbale and cob building near Axminster in east Devon was also refused planning permission, as the application was made under Para 79, a provision in English planning law to allow innovative high-quality designed projects in the countryside. As with the Hebden Bridge project, the applicant and their architects submitted an extensive and well-detailed set of proposals with considerable well-referenced detail of the innovative low-carbon credentials of the building. The proposed house was to use locally sourced materials, with a limecrete and clay floor, a combination of cob and strawbale walls and a hemp fibre insulated thatched roof. The application was refused on the grounds that it wasn't sufficiently innovative! The proposed use of strawbale and cob walling was in fact highly innovative and quite unusual. At the time of writing both these projects will have gone to appeal so the final outcome is not known.

Academic and Scientific Work on SB Construction

There are surprisingly few sources for academic and scientific advice about strawbale building in the UK. Work at Bath University Engineering Department helped to establish ModCell and academics there have continued to be involved in research such as the EU-funded ISOBIO project which includes Bath University as partners. (29)

ISOBIO have developed what they claim is a low-energy highly insulating walling system which includes eight layers including clay plaster, a 'lignicell' panel (compressed strawboard) insulation from Cavac Biofib (*see* Chapter 7), a synthetic airtightness fabric, OSB timber board, and more Biofib insulation in two layers including a rigid board and an external render. It is claimed that this will achieve passivhaus standards and an academic paper also makes claims that this provides good hygric performance, but this is a long way from strawbale building. (30)

Such a complex multi-layered approach to creating an insulating wall systems seems far too academic, despite the involvement of industrial partners. It's unlikely that mainstream builders or self-builders would be interested in something so complex when they could achieve similar thermal results using simple strawbale or hempcrete!

One of the key components in this experiment was a 'Stramit' compressed strawboard and on the ISOBIO website it states that Stramit boards have been used in 300,000 houses in the UK (though this seems highly unlikely). (31) Compressed strawboards were widely used in social housing in the 1970s as they were cheap but many of the projects in which they were used were demolished. It was not possible to find any evidence that Stramit or Straw Resource

Ltd exist in the UK though it is possible that Stramit boards are produced in Australia and the US.

Despite talk of zero carbon and environmental aims, the EU has funded surprisingly few projects that might have advanced low-impact natural building. The ISOBIO project has led to proposals for a clay-based internal retrofit panel and a hemp lime rendered external panel.

UPSTRAW

One EU-funded project, through the Interreg programme, supported the UPSTRAW project of the European Straw Building Association. Their excellent website provides extensive information on strawbale projects throughout Europe including the UK, (32) plus many useful resources about SB building methods and case studies. Strawbale Building UK is an association of a number of organizations concerned with strawbale building. It is registered as a community benefit society and provides a wide range of resources and information for anyone wanting to do some SB building. (33)

Plymouth University is an important centre for research into strawbale and other forms of natural building. They have published a number of research papers, some of which are based on real strawbale buildings, showing how lime renders and timber rainscreens can be effective protection for strawbale walls and how SB can meet energy standards. (34) (35) (36)

References

1. http://buildipedia.com/aec-pros/construction-materials-and-methods/straw-bale-construction?print=1&tmpl=component
2. David Eisenberg, 2014, https://www.strawbuilding.org/Resources/Documents/Strawbale_Construction_Building_Codes.pdf
3. Rikki Nitzkin and Maren Termans, *A Complete Guide to Straw Bale Building* (Permanent Publications, 2020).
4. UPSTRAW, https://strawbalebuildinguk.com/wp-content/uploads/2020/01/Upstraw-Yearbook-2020.pdf
5. http://www.bagstudio.org/cose-una-casa-di-paglia/
6. https://www.modcell.com/
7. https://www.lilac.coop/
8. Tom Woolley, *Low Impact Building: Housing Using Renewable Materials* (Wiley, 2013).
9. https://www.yeotown.com/accommodation/
10. ETA Denmark, European Technical Assessment ETA-13/0204 of 10/11/2015 at rockpanel.co.uk/siteassets/documentation/rockpanel-eta/rockpanel_eta_130204.pdf
11. https://www.northwoodsdesign.co.uk
12. Sanin Dzidic, 2017, 'Fire Resistance of Straw Bale Walls', at https://www.researchgate.net/publication/316463900_Fire_Resistance_of_the_Straw_Bale_Walls
13. Jason Ford, 2009, 'Straw House has Good Fire Resistance', at https://www.theengineer.co.uk/straw-house-has-good-fire-resistance/#:~:text=A%20house%20built%20of%20prefabricated,temperatures%20over%201%2C000%C2%B0C
14. David Arkin, undated, at https://www.strawbale.com/wildfires-straw-bale-construction/
15. Richard Stacy, undated, 'Suffolk Strawbale Cottage', at https://suffolkstrawbaleholidaycottage.wordpress.com/tag/car-tyre-foundations/
16. https://passivehouseplus.co.uk/magazine/new-build/norfolk-straw-bale-cottage-aims-for-passive
17. David Smith, 2018, 'All Bales, No Bills', at https://passivehouseplus.ie/magazine/new-build/all-bales-no-bills
18. Sam and Carol Atkinson, undated, at https://www.oneoffplaces.co.uk/Straw-Bale-Cabin

and https://www.oneoffplaces.co.uk/Straw-Bale-Cottage

19. Claire Lloyd, 2020, '£67k Straw Bale Self Build', at https://www.homebuilding.co.uk/ideas/67k-straw-bale-self-build

20. https://www.exmooryoungvoices.org/

21. https://suffolkstrawbaleholidaycottage.wordpress.com/the-build/

22. https://www.hobbithideaway.co.uk/

23. https://www.loughmardalglamping.ie/

24. Andy Hales, 2020, 'Gwalia Chapel', at https://www.andyhalesead.co.uk/straw-bale-chapel

25. https://wecanbuildourchurch.org.uk/

26. https://www.nationaltrust.org.uk/footprint#

27. https://www.crosbygrangerarchitects.co.uk/expertise/design/footprint/

28. https://www.yorkshirepost.co.uk/news/people/council-refuse-planning-permission-for-house-made-from-straw-bales-and-old-tyres-to-be-built-in-hebden-bridge-3160057

29. http://isobioproject.com/publications/

30. F. Collet, S. Prétot, V. Colson, C.R. Gamble, N. Reuge and C. Lanos, 'Hygric Properties of Materials Used for Isobio Wall Solution for New Buildings', 3rd International Conference on Bio-Based Building Materials, 26–28 June 2019, Belfast, UK.

31. http://isobioproject.com/partners/stramit-international-strawboard-ltd/

32. https://strawbuilding.eu/up-straw-interreg-project/

33. https://strawbalebuildinguk.com/

34. Jim Carfrae, Pieter de Wilde, John Littlewood, Steve Goodhew and Peter Walker, 2009, 'Detailing the Effective Use of Rain-screens to Protect Straw Bale Walls in Combination with Hygroscopic, Breathable Finishes', in *Translating Sustainable Design into Sustainable Construction: Detail Design in Architecture 8, Cardiff, 4–8 September 2009*.

35. S. Emmitt and J. Littlewood (eds), *Translating Sustainable Design into Sustainable Construction: Detail Design in Architecture 8, Cardiff, 4–8 September 2009*, conference proceedings, at https://researchportal.bath.ac.uk/en/publications/translating-sustainable-design-into-sustainable-construction-proc

36. Jim Carfrae and Pieter de Wilde, 2017, 'The Leechwell Garden House: A Passive Solar Dwelling Built from Renewable Materials', at https://strawbalebuildinguk.com/wp-content/uploads/2017/09/Leechwell_Garden_House.pdf

Chapter Six

HEMP AND HEMPCRETE

What is Hemp and Why is it Great for Building?

There is little doubt that hemp and hempcrete provide a range of excellent natural materials for building. It is hard to beat the all-round performance and advantages of hempcrete: it is easy to build with, and it is claimed that a good builder can learn how to use hempcrete in a morning and a self-builder in a day. The raw materials are affordable and the results in terms of thermal performance are as good as you can get from any material. Because of these qualities hempcrete, in particular, has been extensively used, but there are still barriers to its uptake. Some natural building enthusiasts are suspicious of the lime binders as some may include cement; others are worried about the association with cannabis and marijuana.

Hemp fibre insulation materials are discussed elsewhere as they are manufactured materials. Hempcrete, on the other hand, can be made on site from raw materials: chopped-up hemp straw (known as shiv or hurds) is mixed with a lime binder and water,

then cast in shuttering, sprayed or made into blocks or used as an insulating plaster. The hemp hurds are a by-product of processing hemp plants which have been grown for seed, fibre and CBD (cannabidiol). The fibre is a high-value material which can be combined with natural resins to produce a range of composite products which are used for car interiors, in aeroplanes and so on. (1) A hemp and bio-resin corrugated composite panel has been developed for a project at Margent Farm in Cambridgeshire.

Hempcrete can create a very long-lasting, robust and fireproof form of construction which also ensures a healthy indoor environment. Wall construction build-up is much simpler than other systems without needing to use excessively thick walls. It's hard to go wrong with hempcrete though there have been plenty of people determined to make a mess of it by using the wrong materials and ignoring tried and tested solutions.

Using hemp is good for the environment because growing it has many advantages for agriculture: it is potentially a valuable crop for farmers, it helps to clean up the ground by suppressing weeds and it requires very little (if any) fertilizer and pesticides. Farmers still have to obtain a government licence to grow hemp and this has restricted its use.

Hemp fibre and bio-resin experimental corrugated sheet used at Margent Farm, Cambridgeshire.

Britain's imperial maritime prowess was based on hemp ropes and sailcloth, and at one time farmers in the UK and Ireland were required by law to grow and process hemp. Dozens of place names throughout Europe have the word 'hemp' in them, from Hemel Hempstead in the UK to Hennef in Germany, and in towns like Bridport in Dorset many buildings were devoted to hemp processing, with the hemp imported from Italy, Southern Russia and further afield. (2) There is a rope museum in Chatham dockyard in Kent where the hemp rope-making factory, 346m long, was once the longest brick building in the world. There is a Hemp Street in east Belfast where there were booming rope-making businesses.

Growing hemp became illegal in many countries, led by the US, when nylon was invented, in an effort to put hemp out of business. Slowly but surely, hemp is being legalized across the world, but it is a complicated story due to issues around cannabis and CBD pharmaceuticals. There is not enough space in this book to explore this story but it is important to realize that hemp has thousands of uses and hemp shiv for building is only one, and a low-cost product at that. Hemp enthusiasts can become tiresome with their zealotry for hemp but to use hemp and hempcrete

Hemp Street in east Belfast. (Photo: Lisa Ponzoni)

in building you don't have to become an obsessive hemp and cannabis fanatic!

Benefits of Hempcrete

Hemp and lime composite walling provides very good thermal performance and a way of achieving healthy and sustainable buildings. Hemp lime or hempcrete is a lightweight solid walling system often used with timber frames. It can be used in numerous ways: cast around a timber frame with temporary shuttering, sprayed onto temporary or permanent shuttering, or used as blocks or in prefabricated panels. It is also very useful to cast, spray or plaster onto existing masonry walls to retrofit existing buildings.

Hempcrete has been widely used in the UK since the construction of two houses in Haverhill in Suffolk in 2000. The pioneer of hempcrete construction in the UK, architect Ralph Carpenter, (3) was able to demonstrate that the hempcrete houses outperformed two identical houses built with bricks and mineral wool insulation. He worked with the UK Building Research Establishment (BRE) to monitor and evaluate the building of four houses by the Suffolk Housing Society and the report by Tim Yates from 2002 (4) is still one of the best documents about hempcrete. The hemp houses were predicted to have a poorer energy performance but in fact out-performed the brick houses in terms of heating costs.

The BRE Press published a guide to hemp lime construction in 2008 (5) and since then hemp lime has been used in hundreds of buildings, including huge wine and food warehouses, (6) a six-storey university building in Bradford (7) and many private and social houses. There are five- and six-storey hempcrete apartment buildings in Paris and Italy. Hemp housing in Elmswell, Suffolk, was designed by the 2020 RIBA gold medal winners. (8) Hempcrete is increasingly being used to retrofit historic and old masonry buildings. The Gordon Brown Labour government set up the 'Renewable House Programme' with £6.7 million in 2008 and this led

Bradford University Sustainable Enterprise Centre, also known as 'Re:centre', showing hempcrete walls.

to twelve innovative housing projects, mainly using hempcrete, but some with strawbale, wood fibre and sheep's wool. (9)

How to Use Hempcrete

Hempcrete can be used in floors and roofs as well as walls. Hemp shiv, the chopped and dried woody core of the hemp plant, is mixed with a lime binder and water. It sets remarkably quickly and shuttering can be removed within twenty-four hours. It takes a couple of weeks to dry out and longer to gain its full strength as the lime carbonates. Building with hemp and lime is a relatively simple process and can be understood by any good builder with training. One of the attractions of hempcrete is its potential adoption into mainstream construction.

It's important to use the correct mix proportions, though these can vary according to how it is being

Horizontal forced-action mixer run off tractor being used to mix hempcrete. (Photo: Rachel Bevan)

Smaller mixer.
(Photo: Nigel Kermode)

used, and controlling the correct amount of water is also essential. The hemp and lime is normally mixed in a horizontal forced-action mixer and then sprayed or tipped into shuttering and lightly tamped. The mixers illustrated are run off the back of a tractor but smaller free-standing mixers are available. Wall thicknesses can vary from 200mm to 600mm, and as thin as 50mm, onto existing walls. Currently the main source of hemp shiv is in Yorkshire in England. (10)

Specialist lime binders are made in Northern Ireland (11) and Shropshire (12) but some architects and builders use materials imported from France. Hempcrete is very popular with self-builders and environmental activists and the author has run numerous training workshops around the UK and Ireland, Canada, Chile, Poland, The Netherlands and South Africa. A film about a hempcrete house built in Northern Ireland has been viewed thousands of times. (13) Hempcrete buildings are now found all over the world, with significant growth throughout Europe and the US and some interest in India and South Africa. There is some resistance to hempcrete from natural builders in some countries where there are exponents of strawbale and earth building. There is a dislike of the term 'crete' as this is associated with cement and concrete, though lime binders do not need to include cement. Others think that too much lime is used in the hempcrete mix but this is because some hempcrete exponents may have used far too high a proportion of lime to achieve a solid set.

Hempcrete provides insulation that has good thermal mass and is also permeable to water vapour. This means that plastic airtightness membranes are not normally necessary, though they are sometimes used, and the construction build-up is much simpler than in a normal timber frame. While the U value of hempcrete is good enough to pass building regulations, its performance in practice can be much better than predicted due to its thermal mass effect. Hempcrete houses can retain a relative humidity of around 50 per cent all year round and most hempcrete buildings stay at 14–15°C with minimal heating. Hempcrete walls are normally finished with a lime render or rainscreen cladding and it is essential to use breathable finishes and paints.

Hempcrete provides an opportunity to create low-carbon buildings and can easily achieve nearly zero performance. By counting the carbonation of the lime and the carbon sequestration of growing the hemp, it is sometimes claimed to be carbon-negative. Hempcrete construction is cost-competitive with conventional timber frame building, even taking account of the labour costs of installing the hempcrete. Hempcrete has been demonstrated to be very fire-resistant and is a simple way of achieving good indoor air quality. Care should be taken to get the best advice from hempcrete builders and suppliers rather than relying on a growing number of questionable guides on the internet.

Hemp Fibre

Hemp has huge regenerative potential as it has many agricultural benefits, with valuable uses of the fibre, CBD (if legal) and as a food and oil source. Hemp can be grown in most parts of the UK and as it locks up carbon more quickly than some other bio-based materials it can make a huge contribution to the push to reduce CO_2 emissions.

Hemp fibre is one of the strongest plant fibres and is stripped from the plant in a process called decortication. After harvesting the plant is 'retted' to soften the fibres and make it easier to process. There are various ways of doing this and the different processes create different grades and quality of both hemp fibre and shiv, the straw. As this book is concerned with using the materials available for building it is best to look elsewhere for details of the growing, retting and processing of hemp. Hemp fibre is used for rope, cloth and clothing and is stronger than cotton. It can be manufactured as an insulation quilt (often referred to as hemp wool), felted into batts or made into board products and many variations are available (*see* Chapter 7). As with so many natural materials these are largely imported but companies are planning to establish hemp production factories in the UK. Some companies add polyester as a binder and others use cornmeal in hemp fibre insulation, but polyester can be up to 40 per cent of the content of the insulation, which gives it very bad environmental credentials in terms of lifecycle analysis. Flame-retardant chemicals such as ammonium phosphate or soda are often added. Hemp boards are usually made from leftover straw (shiv) and dust and use resins as a bonding agent. As hemp boards are quite dense they do not provide the same level of insulation as hemp fibre quilts and batts.

Hempcrete: Details

Hempcrete, as opposed to manufactured fibre products, has no added chemicals or flame retardants. It is a very unusual material, compared with other insulation products, as it can provide most of the wall, floor or roof construction, normally in conjunction with a timber, steel or concrete structural frame. One of the reasons why hempcrete is not used more widely is because architects, specifiers and their clients find it difficult to understand the completely different concept of building that is hempcrete.

The hemp shiv is mixed with a binder (usually lime-based) and water so that it can be placed in shuttering or sprayed, or made into blocks. Thick solid hempcrete walls with timber frames provide both insulation and a walling system without the need for racking boards, additional insulation or airtightness membranes.

Hempcrete for newbuild is normally cast around a simple timber stud frame. The timber frame can be in the middle or on the inside or outside of the wall. Leaving the studs exposed allows for fixing of a timber rainscreen or other internal fixtures. Conduit for electrical cables and socket boxes can be prefixed and then encased within the hempcrete. It is better to avoid water pipes cast in the hempcrete walls if possible, but heating pipes have been cast into hempcrete walls and floors. Hempcrete can also be cast up against concrete and steel frames though lightweight galvanized steel might be adversely affected by the pH in the lime. Hempcrete can be applied to existing masonry or even timber walls and can also be cast into prefabricated timber panels.

Cast or sprayed hempcrete will provide excellent airtightness, now required under the building regulations, and this can be achieved without the use of plastic membranes. Where membranes have been

Demonstration hempcrete wall (with happy trainees) cast at farm in Co. Kerry; workshop organized by Hemp Co-operative Ireland.

used, this is simply as an extra layer against driving rain behind rainscreen cladding and it is important that membranes or other materials such as permanent shuttering are not used in a way that prevents the hempcrete drying out fully.

Structural Properties

Hempcrete is not generally seen as a load-bearing material, though denser mixes can achieve relatively good compressive strength comparable with weak concrete blocks. Hempcrete is mainly used as an infill insulating and walling material in conjunction with a structural frame provided by timber or other materials. Normally, timber frame buildings use sheathing boards of plywood or OSB to brace the structure but the hempcrete can actually provide the bracing or racking resistance. When constructing a hempcrete building, temporary bracing may be required but as the hempcrete cures and the lime carbonates, the hempcrete can provide racking resistance and will also resist wind shear. According to one engineering MSc thesis, 'Testing ... showed that hempcrete panels have the potential to have similar stiffness to braced panels (although with lower strength)'. (14)

Finishing Hempcrete

Hempcrete should not be left unfinished externally. Externally, it is normal to use a sand and lime render. It is essential to use breathable materials so hempcrete should not be finished with gypsum plasters (if at all possible), nor with plastic paint or cement renders, nor wrapped tightly in plastic membranes. Clay plasters and clay-based paints will work well with hempcrete as well as lime renders and plasters. There should always be an air gap behind rainscreen cladding.

Weathering and Moisture

Having created buildings with cavity walls for many decades, it seems counter-intuitive to create solid wall buildings with one material (hempcrete) all the way through. Providing the external finish has been done well, there have not been reports of dampness penetrating through hempcrete. Where there are reports of dampness with hempcrete this is due to the use of wrong materials and vapour-closed permanent shuttering boards. Hempcrete, like other natural bio-based materials, allows water vapour to pass through the fabric. This does not mean air passing through but the ability of what are known as 'hygroscopic' materials to regulate humidity and moisture. Hempcrete is particularly good in this respect as hemp can cope with wetting and lime has been used for centuries as a way of preserving timber and other things. There are few other construction materials which provide good insulation and can also regulate moisture in this way.

Hempcrete has been used in highly exposed weather situations such as the Isle of Colonsay on the west coast of Scotland. Where there are concerns about driving rain, a timber rainscreen can be used though external renders can be painted with a mineral silicate paint.

Insulation Properties of Hempcrete

As pressure increases to ensure that buildings meet with zero or net carbon standards, officialdom and the industry are moving towards so-called super-insulating materials to provide excellent thermal resistance. Claims about super-insulation are greatly exaggerated and research has revealed a massive performance gap (15) where buildings using conventional construction methods and synthetic insulations can perform up to 70 per cent worse than predicted. Hempcrete, which provides a modest U value of 0.2, is rejected by many as not providing sufficient insulation, but this is because current methods of calculating thermal performance have been designed to favour lightweight synthetic materials while ignoring thermal mass. An explanation about thermal insulation in more detail can be found in the book by Latif *et al.* (2019). (16)

There a number of reasons for the good thermal performance of hempcrete:

1. Thermal comfort: due to the ability of hempcrete to regulate humidity the occupants will feel more comfortable and not tempted to turn up the heat to mitigate the effects of cold walls.
2. Hempcrete maintains steady internal temperatures whatever is happening outside, which means that any additional heating is minimized to raise the temperature to an acceptable level. Cooling should not be required in hot weather.
3. Hempcrete has the enormous benefit of thermal mass while also providing a good level of insulation. Thermal mass is found in earth, concrete and masonry buildings, but without the same level of insulation.
4. To understand this means understanding the 'decrement factor': that is, the process by which certain materials are quicker or slower to heat up or cool down. The time lag with lightweight insulated buildings is quite short and even with super-insulated materials, heat is lost through the fabric surprisingly quickly. With hempcrete the heat loss is so slow that the building retains warmth. Research has shown that in a conventional synthetic-insulated building, internal temperatures mirror the external conditions, whereas in a hempcrete building the temperature stays almost constant. This can also be achieved in straw and earth buildings.
5. When thermal performance is calculated for building regulations using the Standard Assessment Procedure (SAP), thermal mass is barely considered, to the disadvantage of hempcrete.

It is possible to vary the thermal resistance of hempcrete by varying the density. The denser the hempcrete, the stronger it is but the poorer the insulation. It is normal to aim for about 320–350kg/m^3 for hempcrete but by reducing the amount of lime in the mix it can get down as low as 250kg/m^3. Generally, 320kg/m^3 is seen as a happy medium between strength, thermal mass and insulation, and making walls much thicker or less dense may not make very marked changes in the thermal performance.

When considering using hempcrete it is normal to find many detractors who will have a hundred and one reasons for not using hempcrete and the first will be that it provides poor insulation. Some passivhaus assessors, for instance, have insisted on the addition of a layer of polystyrene insulation with hempcrete, leading to serious dampness and mould growth. These energy and passive 'experts' do not seem to understand the importance of thermal mass and the decrement factor. According to one passivhaus pundit, 'the general public's perception is out of all proportion to the ability of thermal mass to reduce heating demand'. (17) This is because many professionals assume that thermal mass is achieved through concrete rather a thermally dynamic material such as hempcrete.

Hemp Shiv

It is important to use the correct kind of shiv for hempcrete. Particle sizes can vary but are normally in the range of 10–25mm in length. The shiv should be largely free of fibre and dust: a little of this does not normally cause problems when casting hempcrete in shuttering, but can be more of a problem when spraying. When spraying hemp, it is important to have a more consistent size of shiv, small enough to go through the spraying machine.

Sources of Hemp Shiv

The two main suppliers of hemp shiv in England are East Yorkshire Hemp (18) and Harrison Spinks. (19) Both companies have many years of experience growing, working with farmers and processing hemp, and are able to produce hemp shiv that is suitable for casting hempcrete. There are numerous other sources of hemp shiv throughout Europe, including France, The Netherlands, Poland, Lithuania and Italy. At the time of writing there is a surplus of hemp and thus imported hemp can be affordable, even with transport costs, though you might prefer hemp that is grown locally. Also, some European hemp processors are able to vary the size of the hemp particle and may provide shiv more suitable for spraying. Other companies are being set up in the UK to process hemp and so there may be other local sources for shiv in the future, though to date it is not yet clear whether these new companies have the expertise to produce good-quality hemp.

There are now many hundreds of farmers growing hemp in both England and Ireland, some in Northern Ireland but fewer in Scotland and Wales. Investment in the machinery for the processing and decortication of the hemp involves a large initial outlay,

Hemp shiv, usually packed in approximately 18kg bags which are, unfortunately, plastic.

Hemp baled by Harrison Spinks from their own farm or from farmers contracted to grow hemp.

Hemp fibre after processing in the decortication machinery; this will be used by Harrison Spinks in the manufacture of mattresses.

Some of the processing machinery in the Harrison Spinks factory in Yorkshire.

and demand in the market for hemp fibre and shiv has not yet developed enough to attract this sort of financial move. There are various small-scale mobile decorticators available which are heavily promoted on the internet, but these are unable to process the quantities of hemp to meet construction needs. Some people assume that they might be able to grow an acre of hemp on their own land and then use it to build with but this is generally impractical.

Alternatives to Hemp

There has been an effort by a few people to replace hemp with miscanthus (elephant grass). This has been grown extensively in eastern England as a bio-mass crop to burn in power stations. Work at Aberystwyth University has been promoting the replacement of hemp with chopped miscanthus; however, while the miscanthus appears to mix with lime much like hempcrete, in practice and in tests carried out in Northern Ireland, it has been found not to be so robust and takes considerably longer to dry out. Hemp works perfectly well so there does not seem to be any logical reason for replacing it with other straws and fibres that are not as robust. An experimental house has been built with miscanthus bales (20) but it was not possible to find much about the real experience of using miscanthus with lime in a similar form to hempcrete, even though it has been used in small quantities for renovation. (21)

Bad Advice about Hempcrete

Hemp does attract many enthusiasts who post a wide range of confusing things on the internet and social media. It is probably advisable to ignore much of this and listen to experienced hemp-building experts by attending a training workshop or reading the hempcrete book! (22) (23) For instance, it is not a good idea to use the whole of the hemp plant for construction as the hemp fibre holds much more water and will make the composite slow to dry out and yet this is promoted by some, despite the failure of walls to dry out. Others advise the wetting of hemp before it is mixed with the lime binder: this is a mistake as it then becomes difficult to control the amount of water in the mix. There is also a great deal of misinformation about lime binders. Do not let this put you off as there is plenty of good advice about hempcrete and it is not difficult to get it right.

Water Ratio

It is important to use the correct ratio of hemp to binder and water. However, this does not mean there is a rigid figure for this. The moisture content of hemp can vary and even the ambient air conditions and humidity can have an effect. The experienced hempcrete builder will know how to control the amount of water added as the hempcrete mix will look too dry until it is placed in the shuttering. Inexperienced builders will tend to add too much water which will wash out the lime, so control of water is critical. Some binder manufacturers will give an indication of the correct amount of water to use.

Lime Binders

There are a wide range of proprietary lime binders on the market and for the inexperienced self-builder or building contractor it is best to use these as, providing the instructions about mix proportions are followed, the results should be satisfactory.

It is possible to create your own binder from raw materials but it is important to weigh and measure materials carefully and stick to the same blend once it has been proved to work. Sadly, some internet and social media pundits suggest that anyone can make up their own binders but the wrong materials may be used and this has led to dampness and failures. However, when working around the world where the ideal materials are not always available it has been possible to make up a satisfactory binder using the local lime available, but this has to be done very carefully.

Normally, lime binders for hempcrete consist of a blend of hydrated lime, hydraulic lime and sometimes a little cement and other additives. There has been criticism of hempcrete by those who disapprove of the use of cement, but much of the world's manufacture of lime products is controlled by the cement industry. Lime binders do not need to include a small amount of cement, even though it can aid the setting process.

It is important to be aware that not all hydrated limes (or air limes) are the same and the quality can vary considerably. Cheap hydrated lime, as produced by cement companies and available from local builders' merchants, is generally unsuitable for use as a binder for hempcrete, though some have tried this and failed. Do not be tempted to buy this cheap hydrated lime and think that you can create good hempcrete with this. Hot lime enthusiasts (*see* Chapter 4) disapprove of hydraulic limes and some are therefore critical of hempcrete, but hot limes would be unsuitable for a hempcrete mix. For a time, some of the proprietary binders contained high levels of cement but this is less clear today when manufacturers use the term 'hydraulic binder' in their data sheets. Cement can be considered to be a 'hydraulic binder'!

The inclusion of cement and other additives is largely to speed up the drying and setting of hempcrete. Often the additives are a trade secret but can include pozzolans and other substances. There is a considerable amount of scientific and engineering academic literature on hempcrete, binders and additives, though this may not be of interest to those wanting to build with the materials. A useful discussion can be found by Pavia and Walker of Trinity College Dublin. (24)

Metakaolin is sometimes proposed as an additive to use with hydrated lime and appears to be successful in use. (25) The use of kaolin and clay as a binder is also being developed but is still largely experimental. The long-term objective should be to eliminate dependence on cement and even reduce the use of lime as this will reduce the embodied energy of the building.

Kilwaughter Minerals is a company based near Larne in Northern Ireland, best known in the construction industry for their cementitious renders and products such as K Rend. However, they have for a number of years produced a lime-based binder for use with hemp which has been successfully used on many hempcrete projects. It is a blend of hydraulic and hydrated lime and other additives. They have produced a data sheet which sets out the appropriate mix proportions (26)

Lime Green Products Ltd are manufacturers and stockists of a wide range of lime and ecological products. They have produced a lime binder for hempcrete at their factory in Shropshire. At the time of writing, information about this product was not readily available but they are working on a data sheet and full listing on their website. This lime binder has been used successfully on a range of hempcrete projects. (27)

There have been a range of Tradical lime binders for hempcrete available for a number of years, produced by the multinational Belgian lime company Lhoist. This product is not manufactured in the UK and must be imported from Europe. Tradical, based in Besançon in eastern France, have changed their formulation several times and now have a range of hempcrete products. They set out a range of mixes in their data sheets, with a range of products such as Tradical Thermo, PF 70, PF 80 M, Batir, Chanvribat and Premium. (28). Tradical claim they can achieve a density for walls of 280 kg/m³. (29)

Batichanvre is a lime binder for hempcrete produced by the French Bordeaux-based company St Astier. Their data sheet shows much higher densities than Tradical. The Batichanvre mix consists of calcium hydroxide and a hydraulic binder which they say is a blend of natural hydraulic lime, hydrated lime, hydraulic binder and additives. The term 'hydraulic binder' can mean cement. (30)

Prompt, sometimes referred to as Roman cement, is a widely used material for many purposes, but is also used for hempcrete. While Vicat, based near Lyon in France, promote their products for use with sprayed hempcrete, it proved difficult to find product data sheets that provided any more detail. (31) Vicat also produce hempcrete blocks, which have been used in the construction of the Pierre Chevet Sports Hall in Croissy-Beaubourg east of Paris, though you would not recognize it as a hempcrete building from the modern cement-fibre external cladding. (32) The blocks are interlocking and no mortars or adhesives were used, it is claimed.

Vicat and Batichanvre products are stocked by a range of lime and eco supplier companies in the UK and Ireland though you may prefer to go directly to France to order the binders. Hempcrete experts can argue for many hours about binders and which to use. Some people prefer to use locally made binders rather than importing from France, but it's important to remember that natural hydraulic limes (if they are part of the formulation) are no longer made in the UK and have to be imported from France, Italy or Portugal. There are other binders available, particularly from Italy and Eastern Europe.

Mixing and Placing Hempcrete

The simplest way to create hempcrete walls is by hand-casting into shuttering. Once the hempcrete has been mixed with the correct amount of water, it can be transported in wheelbarrows and buckets and dropped into shuttering made from a range of strong boards such as OSB or plywood. Once in the shuttering the hempcrete is lightly compressed in a process called tamping. The main purpose of this is to ensure that the shuttering is fully filled and there are no gaps. It is not necessary to compress or vibrate the hempcrete as is done with rammed earth, for instance. Tamping too hard is often raised as a problem but if the hempcrete is correctly mixed it has its own resistance and will not easily be overly compressed. If the shuttering and tamping is done properly then when the shuttering is removed the face of the hempcrete should be smooth and can be left internally unfinished with plaster. Tamping is usually done with any offcuts of wood that are lying about and a special tool is not necessary.

Carting wheelbarrows of hempcrete and placing them into shuttering seems labour-intensive but does not take too long, especially if you have friends and volunteers to help. Setting up the shuttering should be done carefully but not too much is required as lower

Hand placing of hempcrete into shuttering: this may seem labour-intensive as it needs to be done with care, yet it can be done quite quickly.

shutters can be removed and used again as the wall increases in height. In the early days of casting hempcrete, shuttering was designed with heavy plywood and massive bolts but this is not necessary and any second-hand plywood or other boards will do the job, fixed temporarily to the timber frame of the building with screws or bolts. Shuttering can be designed to create curved walls if these are required. Spacers are normally used between the shuttering boards and the timber frame and there are various easy ways to do this.

Shuttering around windows is most easily done by using permanent but breathable boards, such as woodwool, which are then left in position, but there are many options. Completing the casting at the top of walls is the trickiest part as this cannot usually be done with shuttering unless there is access from above. Hempcrete should be nice and sticky and can be placed by hand and smoothed off with a trowel; it can be cast into floors and also prefabricated panels.

Spraying Hempcrete

Hempcrete can be sprayed using specialist machinery and this can be much faster and more efficient than hand-casting. This significantly reduces the need for shuttering, though shuttering on one side may be normal. You can even spray onto breathable permanent shuttering boards. It's also possible to spray onto temporary plastic sheeting which can then be

Mixer and equipment for spraying hempcrete developed by Graham Durrant of Hemp-Lime Spray Ltd.

Spraying hempcrete onto temporary shuttering by one of Graham Durrant's team.

re-used. Some hempcrete will end up on the floor during spraying but most of this 'drop' can be shovelled up and re-used with hand-casting into shuttering in another section of wall not suitable for spraying.

Spraying machines have mostly been developed in France, but exist in the UK. The hemp is placed in a large container and blown down a pipe using a compressor. This is mixed through a special nozzle with a mixture of lime binder and water. A level finish for the sprayed material can be achieved using a laser and the hempcrete is easily scraped back with a board to create a level finish. Placing hempcrete into a roof is most easily achieved using spray machinery, and applying hempcrete onto existing masonry walls can be done by spraying, though casting into temporary shuttering is also possible. (33) Graham Durrant of Hemp-Lime Spray will happily sell you a spraying machine and provide training in how to use it.

Hempcrete Block Construction

Hempcrete can be cast into blocks; while this is not such a good way of making hempcrete walls as casting and spraying it is immediately attractive to many people who find it hard to understand the normal way of casting hempcrete but do understand concrete blocks. Hempcrete blocks need to be glued together with a mortar and still require to be used with some

kind of structural frame. Currently, hempcrete blocks are manufactured in commercial quantities in Belgium, France and Italy (34) (35) (36) and there are those who prefer to import the blocks at great expense across Europe rather than casting hempcrete on site. There are companies talking of producing hempcrete blocks in the UK.

Hempcrete blocks have the advantage that they arrive on site dry and can be installed in the winter when mixing lime may not be advisable in cold weather. A hybrid form of construction has been used with block-built walls which are then sprayed or cast with hempcrete to give better airtightness and thermal performance. Blocks can also be very useful for renovation where mixing wet hempcrete might create a mess in an existing building (as the blocks can be carried upstairs or into less accessible areas).

A worrying development has been with some architects who are designing walls made out of conventional concrete blocks with hempcrete blocks used on the inside or the outside. This is being done because they do not think that hempcrete will cope with adverse weather conditions but also they are viewing the conventional blocks as providing the structure. However, this may to lead to interstitial condensation and dampness problems at the face between the concrete and hempcrete, with the hempcrete not drying out so easily, and this approach is not advised.

Prefabricated hempcrete panels cast on the flat; these will be dried and then lifted to site. (Photo: Will Stanwix)

Italian hempcrete blocks with mortar built into wall. (Photo: Paolo Ronchetti Blocco Ambiente)

Prefabricated Hempcrete

Hempcrete can be cast into a wide range of prefabricated panels and transported to site for quick construction without the need to wait for the hempcrete to dry out. A small number of projects have been done like this in the UK, but this has been more widely used in Europe. Ideally, the panels should be designed to avoid a wood-to-wood joint between panels and there are various ways to achieve the continuity of hempcrete, thus reducing risks of cold bridging and poorer airtightness. Some prefabricated hempcrete buildings are wrapped in plastic membranes and sticky tape but this rather defeats the object of using hempcrete as the breathability, thermal lag and humidity-controlling properties of the material are partially lost.

Prefabricated panels are usually made on their backs and the hempcrete cast or sprayed between the timber, onto either temporary or permanent breathable shuttering boards. Hempcrete, if properly mixed, should not shrink away from the timber and once dry seems subject to suffer little, if any, damage when transported from place to place. As mainstream house building is moving more towards structural insulated panels (SIPs) and other forms of prefabrication, hempcrete may be used in this way in the future for mass housing.

Multi-Storey and Large Buildings

Hempcrete has been used in a number of five- and six-storey buildings, including university and government offices and apartments. It has also been used in large food and wine storage warehouses and a Marks & Spencer superstore at Ellesmere Port in Cheshire. Casting, spraying or using hempcrete blocks for infill in multi-storey building construction could solve many of the current problems with fire safety, insulation and overheating in such structures. An important hempcrete project is the Rediscovery Centre in Ballymun in Dublin. Funded by the EU Life programme and Dublin City Council, an old boiler house was repurposed into an environmental education and recycling centre. Much of the original building was re-used and the main walls were insulated with hempcrete. Some salvaged sheep's wool was also used and wood fibre boards were used to line an old brick wall. The hempcrete was only partially plastered internally

The Rediscovery Centre in Ballymun, Dublin: conversion of old boilerhouse using hempcrete.

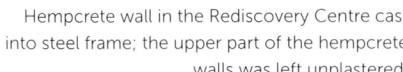

Hempcrete wall in the Rediscovery Centre cast into steel frame; the upper part of the hempcrete walls was left unplastered.

so it could be seen by visitors, but also because this produced better acoustic properties. The hempcrete has a timber subframe but was also cast into the steel-framed structure.

Certification and Standards

A common excuse among mainstream architects and builders for not using hempcrete is the absence of certification and approved standards. This problem applies to many natural materials, particularly those that are fabricated on site. Increasing demands for paper trails for materials and products creates enormous amount of bureaucracy and work for 'experts' who rarely get out from behind their computers. There are frequent demands for lifecycle analysis and embodied-energy calculations for hempcrete, even though its impact on the environment is so much better than conventional synthetic materials. With much talk of the circular economy there are complaints that hempcrete cannot be recycled at the end of its life. This ignores the fact that hempcrete is likely to last a lot longer than many lightweight materials and it can be returned to the earth at the end of its life as hemp can compost and lime can enrich the soil (providing there is minimal cement contamination).

Hempcrete can lock up CO_2 in a building and so is not just zero-carbon but carbon-negative. There are numerous academic studies that address these issues and a new hempcrete book that makes reference to these should be available in a year or two.

There are few certificates and standards that exist for hempcrete. Demands for Environmental Product Declarations (EPDs) and Agrément certificates may not be met, but Local Authority Building Standards Approval (LABSS) has been obtained in Scotland. (37). The Rediscovery Centre in Dublin, the biggest hempcrete building in Ireland, received a fire certificate and was readily accepted by Dublin City Council. As hempcrete is more widely used throughout Europe, certification and standards will become more common. Hempcrete in France has been in use for thirty years or more and there are extensive standards and approvals through bodies like Construire En Chanvre. (38)

Embodied-energy calculations are often requested and obtaining independently certified calculations for this may be difficult though figures are available. Hempcrete is missing from some embodied energy and LCA (lifecycle assessment) data bases and tools but this is slowly being corrected.

Because hempcrete performs so much better in all of these respects than conventional building materials, it can seem rather tedious to hemp building enthusiasts to have to spend valuable time doing theoretical calculations when they could be building instead!

Fire Performance of Hempcrete

Most synthetic insulation materials are flammable, even those which claim not to be. Wood fibre and strawbale are relatively fire-safe, but hempcrete provides a good level of fire performance. As with so many other aspects of hemp there is an absence of paper fire certificates but hempcrete has been shown in fire tests to last more than an hour. Perhaps the best proof of this was a serious fire in a lean-to part of a hempcrete cottage in Devon, which was attended by six fire engines. While there is some scorching apparent, the hempcrete prevented the spread of the fire to the rest of the house. In a structural report for insurance purposes following the fire, the engineer stated:

> The performance of the Hempcrete wall infill does appear to have been largely resistant to the effects of the fire, and any ingress of water following fire suppression has naturally ventilated due to the vapour permeability of the material.

Hempcrete is naturally resistant to fire, and the system, when tested, does meet the requirements of BS EN 1364-1:2015, Fire resistance tests for non-loadbearing elements. It is apparent that the hempcrete has performed as expected, offering adequate fire protection. The damage sustained to the hempcrete is largely due to the actions of the Fire Service to ensure that any hot spots or suspected voids within the hempcrete walls were excavated. (39)

Colin Souch, the engineer who wrote this report, indicated in email correspondence that there had been some shrinkage in the building due to the use of green oak timber frames but this can also be a problem with ordinary softwood frames and any shrinkage gaps could have created a fire path through the hempcrete. The fire brigade damaged some of the hempcrete to ensure that there were no hot spots around the timber frame but this was not a problem. Careful detailing of hempcrete should avoid these problems, as shrinkage in hempcrete is rare but there can be movement caused by the timber frame. Overall, the hempcrete was largely untouched and was easily repaired.

In Drewsteignton (Devon), a fire caused by a faulty electrical appliance in a lean-to structure which was part of a hempcrete cottage: the fire was attended by six fire appliances. (Photo: Spencer Smith)

Acoustic Properties

Hempcrete provides excellent acoustic performance as it acts as a sound absorber when used both internally and externally. (40)

Hemp Clay and Earth

The CobBauge Project, where hemp and clay has been mixed to create very thick walls, has been discussed in Chapter 2. Experimental work on using metakaolin and kaolin powder binders instead of lime is proceeding but to date not enough is known about the robustness of this composite. However, there may be an option in the future to reduce the embodied energy of hempcrete by using clay or a mix of clay and lime.

Hempcrete Retrofit

Examples of hempcrete used in renovating old buildings are shown in Chapter 9. It is surprising how even a thin layer of hempcrete 50–75mm thick, cast with a temporary or permanent timber frame, can make a significant difference to the thermal and humidity performance of a space. Thus, a relatively thin layer of hempcrete can be used to improve air quality in most buildings.

Fire-damaged hempcrete house at Drewsteignton being repaired. (Photo: Spencer Smith)

Experimental wall sections made with hemp and kaolin; one of these has been left un-rendered in the rain for four years and has suffered little deterioration.

Timber rainscreen covers hemp and earth walls at house in Fife, Scotland. (Photo: Tom Morton, Arc Architects)

Hempcrete Project Examples

There are thousands of hempcrete buildings in the UK and the following examples have been chosen to illustrate different aspects.

On Colonsay in Scotland, a house was designed and built by Native Architects of York in collaboration with the Hemp-Lime Spray company: it is in a very exposed location on this island off the west coast of Scotland where it is likely to get a great deal of rainfall. The house includes hempcrete floors. Shipping hempcrete to a Scottish island means transporting far less weight than shipping concrete or concrete blocks.

Designed by Practice Architects, the Flat House at Margent Farm, Cambridgeshire, was built with prefabricated panels by William Stanwix, incorporating a range of other innovative features including hemp fibre composite cladding. The interior hempcrete was left unplastered.

The firm of East Yorkshire Hemp grows and processes hemp and supplies hemp shiv for building projects. The farmhouse built by Keith Voase, the owner of the company, has featured on BBC TV's *Countryfile* programme. Not far away in Leeds and Tadcaster, the enterprise of bed manufacturers Harrison Spinks has incorporated hemp into their mattress products.

Only 50mm of cast hempcrete has been used in this timber cabin to provide insulation but to also help buffer humidity and reduce damp.

Casting hempcrete floor in new house built on Colonsay. (Photo: Native Architects)

General view of hempcrete house on Colonsay under construction. (Photo: Native Architects)

The Flat House at Margent Farm, Cambridgeshire, built with prefabricated hempcrete panels and using innovative hemp fibre composite rainscreen designed by Paloma Gormley of Practice Architecture and hempcrete constructed by Will Stanwix. (Photo: David Grandorge)

The Flat House, interior. (Photo: David Grandorge)

The Flat House, interior. (Photo: David Grandorge)

This has helped to make Yorkshire the main centre for hemp production in the UK currently.

House built by East Yorkshire Hemp, one of the main processors and suppliers of hemp in the UK along with Harrison Spinks. (Photo: East Yorkshire Hemp)

Small hempcrete building at Cae Mabon, a retreat centre in Snowdonia, Wales; much of the hempcrete was installed by volunteers in bad weather in their Easter volunteer week. (Photo: Eric Maddern)

Cae Mabon is a retreat centre in Snowdonia, North Wales, that features a big range of natural buildings, including this small hempcrete cabin. The hempcrete work was done over a very few cold days by volunteers at temperatures that would normally be considered unsuitable for making hempcrete, but the walls were fine.

The Galloway hempcrete house with lime render partially complete and some timber rainscreen cladding. (Photo: Garry Turnbull)

Isle of Man stone building after hempcrete work completed. (Photo: Darren Jackson)

Old stone building in the Isle of Man about to be renovated with hempcrete. (Photo: Darren Jackson)

These before-and-after shots of stone-building retrofit in the Isle of Man demonstrate how hempcrete can be used with masonry buildings that are not in a good condition, to create a modern warm interior.

This timber-frame hempcrete house in Galloway is being constructed in 2021 by a local builder, George Shaw, and Hemp-Lime Spray from Norfolk, using a

Timber frame house in Galloway, Scotland, constructed by local contractor George Shaw and using hempcrete by Hemp-Lime Spray. Architect Rachel Bevan (Photo: Garry Turnbull)

Detail of Galloway house, showing use of temporary shuttering and permanent wood wool shuttering around window openings. (Photo: Garry Turnbull)

Hemp Cottage, Co. Down, under construction. Architect Rachel Bevan (Photo: Rachel Bevan)

Hemp Cottage, completed. (Photo: Rachel Bevan)

post and beam timber frame with sprayed hempcrete. The hempcrete was sprayed onto temporary plastic shuttering but some of the walls were also cast by hand. The structure was designed by Rachel Bevan Architects.

Situated in Crossgar, County Down, Northern Ireland, Hemp Cottage is well known to the many thousands who have viewed the YouTube video of its construction and other subsequent TV programmes. Designed by Rachel Bevan Architects, it is let as a holiday cottage and a number of visitors have gone on to build their own hempcrete houses.

References

1. https://eiha.org/media/2014/10/European-Hemp-fibres-for-diverse-bio-based-products-2010.pdf
2. https://historicengland.org.uk/images-books/publications/bridport-and-west-bay/
3. https://www.modece.com/
4. https://projects.bre.co.uk/hemphomes/HempHousesatHaverhillfinal.pdf
5. https://www.brebookshop.com/details.jsp?id=325431
6. https://www.vincent-gorbing.co.uk/architecture/the-wine-society
7. https://www.bradford.ac.uk/estates/capital-projects/completed-projects/sec/
8. http://www.mikhailriches.com/project/clay-fields/#slide-2
9. https://www.wiley.com/en-gb/Low+Impact+Building:+Housing+using+Renewable+Materials-p-9781444336603
10. https://www.harrisonspinks.co.uk/news-press/harrison-spinks-ecoshiv
11. https://www.k-rend.co.uk/products/k-lime/hemp-lime-binder)
12. Lime Green, https://www.lime-green.co.uk/
13. https://www.youtube.com/watch?v=zOVNlKXxEBw
14. J. G. Winterbottom, 'How should the Racking Resistance of Hempcrete Infill Panels in an Historic Timber Frame be Assessed?' Weald and Downland Museum, University of York MSc thesis, 2021.
15. https://www.zerocarbonhub.org/current-projects/performance-gap
16. Eshrar Latif, Rachel Bevan and Tom Woolley, *Thermal Insulation Materials for Building Applications* (ICE Publishing, 2019).
17. http://www.highlandpassive.com/index.php/how-much-does-mass-matter/
18. https://eastyorkshirehemp.co.uk/
19. https://www.harrisonspinks.co.uk/news-press/harrison-spinks-ecoshiv
20. https://www.aber.ac.uk/en/news/archive/2017/09/title-206144-en.html
21. https://www.addasu.co.uk/case-study/
22. https://carbon.coop/2019/04/using-hemp-lime-for-natural-insulation/
23. William Stanwix and Alex Sparrow, *The Hempcrete Book* (Green Books, 2014).
24. Rosanne Walker and Sara Pavia, 'Influence of the Type of Binder on the Properties of Lime-Hemp Concrete', *2nd International Conference on Construction and Building Research, Valencia, Spain, 14–16 November 2012.*
25. R. Eires, 'New Eco-friendly Hybrid Composite Materials for Civil Construction', *European Conference on Composites Materials, 12, Biarritz, 2006.*
26. https://kilwaughter.com/
27. Lime Green Products Ltd, at https://m.facebook.com/LimeGreenProductsLtd/photos/a.1556958921286621/2510962855886218/?type=3&__tn__=-R
28. https://www.bcb-tradical.com/en/hempcrete/
29. https://www.bcb-tradical.com/wp-content/uploads/2018/02/Tradical-Thermo-technical-data-sheet.pdf
30. http://www.stastier.co.uk/nhl/data/pdfs/batichanvre.pdf
31. https://www.vicat.com/our-solutions/our-realization/individual-and-collective-housing/sprayed-hempcrete-fills-place-eco
32. https://www.dezeen.com/2021/08/01/hemp-crete-pierre-chevet-sports-hall-lemoal-lemoal/
33. http://hemplimespray.co.uk/
34. https://www.isohemp.com/en/hemp-blocks-naturally-efficient-masonry
35. https://tecnocanapa-bioedilizia.it/blocco-ambiente/
36. https://www.hempbuild.ie/hempbuild-qualified-hempcrete-installation
37. https://www.labss.org/hempcrete
38. https://www.construire-en-chanvre.fr/documentation#regles_professionnelles
39. PCA Consulting Engineers Ltd, Structural Report, Froggy Villa Drewsteignton, October 2017, unpublished.
40. https://www.euronoise2018.eu/docs/papers/255_Euronoise2018.pdf

Chapter Seven

MANUFACTURED NATURAL MATERIALS

There are a wide range of manufactured natural building products; however, many are more natural than others, as a number of them have chemicals added to them as glues, binders, preservatives and flame retardants. This chapter may help you sort the sheep from the goats, or the wool from the polyester! As far as possible, companies discussed here were spoken to, and/or information on websites and data sheets was carefully checked. No companies provided any incentives or inducements where more positive comments might be detected. Some of this information may be out of date in the near future but the aim here is to give an analysis of the health and scope of the natural building supply industry at the time of writing, which may grow and improve in the future.

If you do not want to build with materials that have to be fabricated on site such as hempcrete, straw or clay, then buying ready-made products appears to be a good solution. However, you will need to take care in selecting materials, and they are not always as easy to get hold of as they should be. There is also a great deal of misleading marketing and technical information and not all manufacturers and suppliers are as ethical and committed to the environmental aims set out in this book as they should be!

The bulk of manufactured natural materials are insulation quilts and boards, mostly to use in timber frame newbuild construction. There are quite a few other materials, particularly from recycled sources, that are also considered by some to be 'natural'. Many natural materials can be used to renovate existing buildings and indeed are better than conventional synthetic products. However, care has to be taken not to use natural materials in the wrong place. For instance, you would not put sheep's wool under a concrete floor and many natural insulations are unsuitable for masonry cavities.

Providing you use natural-based products, following the manufacturers' instructions, there are a wide range of excellent products available today, far more than when my first *Natural Building* book was written in 2006. (1) You do not need to compromise by using synthetic materials as many jobs can be done with a natural alternative. As competition increases some prices are coming down, while the costs of many conventional building products are rising, and so natural building does not need to be the most expensive option. You can aim to create a nearly plastic- and toxic-free building that will be healthier and often perform better than one made with conventional materials.

Before reviewing the range of materials available it is necessary to address a few problems and obstacles that might discourage you. Unfortunately, due to the lack of interest in natural materials in the UK, the bulk of manufactured materials are imported from mainland Europe. The processing of timber and wood waste is extensive in many European countries, but not in the UK and Ireland. This often means that these products are more expensive than they need to be, even though the basic resources used to make them are not. The departure of the UK from the EU may make the availability of such materials even more problematic. Many of these materials and products could easily be made in the UK and Ireland but the love affair with petrochemical and plastic materials leads many to argue that there is no market for natural materials, and so there has been little investment in production. The detractors of natural materials argue that natural materials are too expensive, not readily available, builders don't know how to use them and that they are not safe and robust, but the wide range of materials and suppliers discussed in this chapter contradicts this.

Sourcing Products

There are a wide range of manufactured natural products, as listed below, but it is important to make an informed choice about the best available. This can be pragmatic or based on cost, or you may prefer to use those that are ethical and environmentally responsible, as many of the suppliers listed here have clear and principled aims that go beyond purely commercial objectives.

Other companies producing or selling the natural products listed below are doing so for purely commercial reasons. They will extol the environmental benefits as part of their marketing strategy, but a little bit of research into the parent companies may raise questions in the minds of those concerned with ethical and environmental aims. If the materials are only what you need then this might not concern you, but there are suppliers whom you may feel more comfortable with from a principled point of view. If ethical and environmental principles are important to you then it is always worth looking up who owns a company and what other interests they have. This can easily be done online through free websites like Company Check (2) but companies come and go and directors disappear and re-appear, so you have to try various search names.

For example, Black Mountain Insulation, selling sheep's wool and hemp products, has an interesting history of ownership and provenance. At the time of writing, it appears to be owned by family members (3) who are also directors of a company called International Petroleum Products (4) which lists a number of petrochemical-based products on its website, such as Ballytherm PIR insulation. (5) A natural wood fibre insulation product called Pavatex is now owned by Soprema, a 100-year-old company specializing in synthetic, plastic and bituminous roofing membranes.

(6) Opinions vary about whether it is a good or a bad thing for natural products to be produced by companies dealing in petrochemical products. Some argue that it is positive that mainstream industry is taking such an interest; on the other hand it may pose a risk of dilution of the natural and environmental credentials of the product and the ownerships outlined above do not necessarily reflect on the quality of the products.

Given the rapid change of ownership in businesses in the construction sector, some of the following information could be well out of date by the time you read this. Takeovers and consolidations are all part of the normal cut and thrust of capitalist business and many natural and ecological materials have been snapped up by companies for purely commercial reasons rather than because they want to save the planet! However, this should give you a good idea of what is available, even if the suppliers have changed.

Challenges in Sourcing Materials

A further problem concerns the distribution and availability of materials and products. You might decide after reading this book that you want to use a particular material or product only to find it is difficult to obtain. This is in part due to the way in which the building materials industry is structured. You may find it next to impossible to order many of the natural materials below from your local builders' merchant or DIY store. Some of the bigger DIY stores used to stock a number of natural materials such as wool and hemp insulation, but no longer do so. After speaking to the B&Q Good Relations PR company in December 2020, to ask them why B&Q no longer stocked natural insulation materials, they were unable to find anyone who could answer this question despite repeated reminders. B&Q is owned by Kingfisher who also own Screwfix, who claim to have a 'responsible business policy' and state on their website that they are responding to demand from customers for more sustainable products. (7) Kingfisher was also unable to provide anyone to answer questions about why they do not stock natural materials.

The building materials market in the UK is dominated by the French Saint Gobain group. They control the bulk of gypsum plasterboard and glass manufacture in the UK and dominate the manufacture of synthetic insulations, including the Celotex that burned on Grenfell Tower. (8) Saint Gobain own Jewsons, Grahams, Weber, JP Corry and many more. Travis Perkins is their main rival and now owns the Wickes DIY stores. There are not many independents and most of them, like the big companies, do not stock natural materials. Despite the apparently competitive nature of commercial business, there is extensive collaboration in the construction materials market and it is not unusual to find the main builders' merchants stocking competitors' products. The insulation market, in particular, is dominated by a small group of companies that either own or distribute products and they can control pricing and distribution. This is partly how they have been able to squeeze out or limit the availability of natural products.

One of the biggest distributors is SIG (previously known as Sheffield Insulation Group) who work with a range of competitors who supply synthetic insulation materials such as Knauf, Recticel, Actis, Celotex, Isover, Kingspan, Rockwool and Superglass. The SIG website is a useful source of information, such as the massive price rises in synthetic insulation over the past few years. Another large company, Encon, did supply sheep's wool insulation at one time (2012) but do not seem to do any longer. (9)

If searching on the internet for natural insulation materials you may stumble across sites such as Insulation Superstore and Insulation4less. They advertise a wide range of synthetic insulations but also a handful of eco products. However, Insulation Superstore, owned by CMO Stores in Plymouth, (10) acts as a contact point for other suppliers, and you might find their website useful for comparing prices. One of the reasons for the high costs of building materials is the structure of middlemen who take a cut but don't hold any stock. You should be able to save money if you go direct to the source, but often these companies, who will be shipping the material to you anyway, still insist you go through a local merchant or distributor for payment.

Sadly, the UK still lacks the existence of holistic manufacturing and material-selling companies that exist in France. Biofib and their sister company Cavac, based in the Loire area of France, advertise a wonderful range of natural insulation products, construction solutions and hempcrete materials. (11) (12) When contacted, Biofib said it was not worth their while exporting to the UK as they thought there wasn't the same level of interest in natural materials as in France. If only such companies existed in the UK and Ireland, life would be so much easier for the aspiring natural builder.

Ecomerchant are the largest players in the UK market: they are committed to ecological principles

Natural insulation from Biofib in France. (Photo: Biofib)

and are in a position to compete with and work with the mainstream companies. In business for twenty-three years, they are exclusive distributors for products such as Steico wood fibre boards and a third of their business is selling to ordinary builders' merchants. You might be able to find sheep's wool or wood fibre products at your local builders' merchant or online retailers but it may be coming from Ecomerchant. (13) As well as selling products the company provides advice, and their website contains a considerable amount of information, as well as a regular blog and technical advice about environmental principles that you will not find from conventional builders' merchants. It is strange that other organizations like Ecomerchant have not emerged.

Many so-called green and eco building suppliers who claim to supply sustainable products turn out to be selling technology such as heat pumps and solar panels, not natural building materials, and will not be much help if you are trying to buy insulation. Some companies are also overcharging for VAT on energy-efficient products, as products like insulation are only meant to be charged at 5 per cent, while nearly all companies are charging 20 per cent VAT to their customers. (14) Getting advice from the HMRC VAT office about this is not easy and there seems to be a great deal of confusion as to what constitutes an energy-efficient product. PVC conservatory roofing sheets are charged at 5 per cent VAT but you may have to pay 20 per cent for much more sustainable materials.

A good check before choosing a product is to ensure that the full technical data about the product is made available. This should be downloadable from the supplier's website. This may consist of an Agrément certificate or a technical data sheet, an environmental product declaration (EPD) plus a COSHH health and safety data sheet, which should include any chemical contents. You will be surprised how often this essential technical data is missing from manufacturers' websites!

Standards and Certification for Products and Materials

Not all eco materials are covered by standards and certificates. Local authorities and building control may insist on sight of certificates and architects are keen for warranties and guarantees to be available. While standards and certification are important to ensure consumer protection, it is the bigger companies that can afford the high costs of the testing and approvals from the British Board of Agrément (15) and KIWA in The Netherlands. (16) Certification should cover fire safety, toxicity, lifecycle and the circular economy and may involve British (BSI) and international standards (ISO). There are a growing number of environmental standards such as Natureplus and a wide variety of eco labels. This can appear to be a bit of a jungle and it does not mean that some products made by local companies, that cannot afford the certification process, are unsatisfactory. Natureplus, based in Germany, has been the leader in setting an ecological gold standard for products with minimal petrochemical and toxic input. (17) However, there are many other European ecological labels.

In the UK, it's worth looking out for LABC (Local Authority Building Control) (18) and LABSS (Local Authority Building Standards Scotland) (19) approval as this is a lower cost system, though it still relies on products having other approvals! When including claims to meet sustainability criteria in planning applications, the planners may be looking for compliance with a standard such as the BRE Green Guide to Specification. However, it may not get you very far if you point out to the planning officer that the BRE Green Guide gives better ratings to petrochemical materials than many ecological products and is in any case produced by a private commercial body, partly funded by the building materials industry. (20)

On-site fabrication of natural materials such as earth and straw can fall outside the scope of many standard certification systems, but this does not mean we should not have standards to ensure that building is done correctly with such materials. However, as it is easier to provide paper trails for manufactured materials, these may often be preferred when making building regulation applications.

Specialist Producers, Stockists and Distributors of Natural Building Materials

There are a handful of specialist eco builders' merchants, some of whom have been in business for many years and are committed to the environmental benefits of their products; if you are new to this, they would be the best people to go to. However, even some of these companies can have blind spots, so you really need to shop around to find what you want and get the best deal. Some companies have exclusive deals with particular manufacturers and this can limit the range of products available. One particular frustration has been the unwillingness of many of the companies listed below to stock hemp and lime binders for hempcrete for instance, though some, if pressed, will agree to supply these materials. You will also find there is interaction and collaboration between some of these companies, stocking similar products but at different prices. The websites for these companies can be found at the end of this chapter and are listed only in alphabetical order for convenience.

These are referred to here as examples of the diversity of suppliers and products that are available and with the ability to search on the internet today you will soon find other new companies and up to date information where contact details have changed. Again, web contact details are listed at the end of this chapter.

England and Wales

There are a number of well-established natural materials suppliers, including Mike Wye, based in mid-Devon, who has been in business for many years and stocks a wide range of lime and natural materials,

insulations, paints and so on. Back to Earth is also in Devon, smaller than Mike Wye, but they offer a lot of technical advice on their website. Celtic Sustainables are based near Cardigan in mid-Wales and stock a wide range of materials. Tŷ-Mawr in Brecon, South Wales, are mainly focussed on lime and historic building materials but also supply insulation and board materials. Womersleys in West Yorkshire tend to focus on limes and materials for historic buildings but do stock a range of insulation and other eco products. Best of Lime in Suffolk is mainly a lime product company but they do stock other materials; they have some interesting plastering and rendering materials. Lime Green in Shropshire has specialized in lime and has recently invested heavily in a major batching plant to blend a range of lime and hempcrete products. They sell a range of insulation materials and a wood fibre building system called Warmshell.

Lime Green's highly sophisticated batching plant allows them to mix different blends of limes and aggregates.

Unity Lime has a base in Yorkshire and also took over the old Natural Building Technologies premises in Buckinghamshire. They stock a range of insulation materials (and a synthetic plastic extruded polystyrene insulation for plinth and perimeter boards). Ecological Building Systems, based in Ireland and Carlisle in England deal in a wide range of natural products from a range of manufacturers including imported products such as Gutex, Finsa and Thermonatur. Ecological Building Systems promote passivhaus and thus also stock a range of plastic and synthetic materials. Ecomerchant are based at the National Self-Build Centre in Swindon but have several other addresses including Stoke-on-Trent and Sittingbourne in Kent. They say they are an 'ethical trading company' part-owned by a 'charitable foundation' which runs a primary school in Burkina Faso. (21) As well as selling wood fibre and sheep's wool they have the exclusive agency for some products such as Lindab guttering, paints and roofing materials and Steico products. One of the biggest players in sustainable building product distribution, it was originally set up by Burdens, a Bristol-based civil engineering company, now owned by Wolseleys (a US multinational).

Green Building Store in Huddersfield is also mentioned here, as they may attract your attention due to their name. However, they do not stock natural building materials as they are committed to passivhaus and only offer plastic foam insulation and technology items like mechanical ventilation and heat recovery systems They do supply imported high-performance triple-glazed timber windows.

Ireland and Northern Ireland

Ireland is quite limited in the number of natural materials suppliers; some operate throughout the UK as well, such as Ecological Building Systems referred to above. Acara Concepts, based in Dublin, supply materials throughout the UK and Ireland. They mainly specialize in imported soundproofing and acoustic products and also supply wood fibre insulation

materials. Heritage Ltd in Northern Ireland specialize in lime and restoration but stock a range of insulation, paints and other products and at the time of writing are setting up a new company called Eco Build Ireland. Stoneware Studios in Cork supply lime, cork, insulations and paints. Roundtower in Cork are mainly lime suppliers but offer a range of other products including insulation and various insulation boards. Sheep Wool Insulation are based in Wicklow in Ireland but sell through a range of distributors in England and Ireland; they are the agents for Isolena sheep's wool in Austria.

Scotland

Strangely, Scotland is barren territory for natural insulations and eco building products and merchants. Some architects in Scotland say that they do not use natural materials due to the severe weather conditions in Scotland but there are many excellent natural building projects in Scotland featured in this book, where the builders have had to source most materials from England. The Scottish Lime Centre provides advice and training and may signpost you to commercial lime suppliers. Masons Mortar in Edinburgh supplies lime. North Woods Design is a timber construction company in the far north of Scotland (featured elsewhere in this book); they might be able to help in sourcing eco materials. There are numerous timber frame companies in Scotland as timber frame building has been well established in Scotland for some years.

Natural Materials with Limited Chemical Additives and Limited Energy Use

The following products and materials are largely natural, combined with other materials or from recycled sources. Most should be available from the sources above or directly from the manufacturers. It is important to distinguish between products which are largely free of synthetic and chemical additives and those listed later which are compromised by less natural substances.

Sheep's Wool

Some sheep's wool products contain plastic materials and chemicals, though when you see the details below you may still be happy to use them as an alternative to entirely petrochemical-based insulations. There is one natural sheep's wool product: Isolena sheep's wool also known as Lehner, based in Austria and Switzerland. They claim to be the only chemical-free sheep's wool product on the market made from 100 per cent sheep's wool, with extensive ecological certification from DGNB (German Sustainable Building Council) and Natureplus in Germany. They use a form of treatment called Ionic Protect rather than chemicals to guard against moths by starving the moths of any food in the wool, thus avoiding biocides. Isolena provides transparent technical information on its website. The stand-alone wool has Class D fire certification but is safer when enclosed with other materials such as plasterboard. Isolena is sold in the UK and Ireland as 'Sheep Wool' insulation.

Isolena Factory in Waizenkirchen, Austria. (Photo: Isolena)

Isolena Sheep Wool installed in timber frame. (Photo: Isolena)

Isolena Sheep Wool installed. (Photo: Isolena)

Isolena Sheep Wool insulation roll. (Photo: Isolena)

There has been some negative propaganda against sheep's wool that it is easily contaminated with moths. There is no doubt that moth infestations have occurred as a result of moths being introduced from other items such as carpets but there are many projects where sheep's wool insulation has been used without any problems with moths. Care should be taken to avoid using sheep's wool insulation in damp conditions such as placing it directly against damp masonry walls or sealing it into dry lining with synthetic boards that are non-permeable to water vapour.

Cork

Cork is available in two main forms, either as expanded insulation boards or as a cork lime composite plaster. Cork tiles are available for flooring and as a decorative finish. There are also cork granules that can be used in floors and cavity walls and a composite product combined with coconut fibre. There is even a cork board product that can be used for external cladding. There are a range of acoustic boards made from cork with either natural or recycled rubber. Some products made from cork waste may be made with a chemical binder such as polyurethane but there are chemical-free versions. Some cork boards are expanded using a super-heated steam system which causes the cork granules to bind together.

Composite cork lime plasters can be hand-applied or sprayed. There are examples of where it is promoted as an alternative to hempcrete but this is a case of comparing apples with pears. Casting a wall 300–400mm thick with hempcrete is affordable but it would not be possible to do this with cork lime. However, a cork lime plaster of 25–50mm will substantially improve thermal comfort, particularly in an old building, and will be comparable with a similar thickness of hemp lime insulation. Cork lime performance as an insulating plaster is also vapour-permeable and hygroscopic, and may help to regulate humidity. Thermal insulation boards are made from waste cork and can range in density from approximately 115 to 160kg/m^3 and be available in a range of sizes, with thicknesses of up to 320mm. It is a good thermal insulator and has good thermal mass. A house has been constructed from solid load-bearing cork panels. (22)

Cork products are available from Amorim who make a range of cork products: they are a Portuguese company in Mozelos near Porto but produce a range of products in other European countries. Diathonite Evolution is a premixed plaster made with hydraulic lime, NHL 3.5, cork, clay, diatomaceous earth and

Interior of cork house. (Photo: Ricky Jones)

External view of house built from solid cork. Collaboration of CSK Architects, Matthew Barnet Howland and Amorim UK and others. (Photo: Ricky Jones)

reinforcing fibres made by Diasen, located in Sassoferrato in Italy; there is a good range of technical literature on their website. Secil Ecocork is a cork lime lightweight render from Secil Argamassass, based in Montijo near Lisbon. Secil Portugal is a producer of hydraulic lime as well as cork products; they claim a thermal conductivity of 0.10 in one document but it proved difficult to access much technical literature. However, there is an LABC certificate for a composite external wall insulation system using hollow clay blocks with cork.

Hemp Fibre and Jute

Despite being some of the best materials for insulation quilts there are very few hemp, flax and jute products available. Bioizol, based in Brno in the Czech Republic, also produces Bio Flex, Canna and Naturizol, though limited information was available about these products. When contacted they said they did have a distributor in the UK but this no longer seemed to be the case at the time of writing. ThermoNatur, based in Nordlingen in Bavaria in Germany, has been taken over by Hempflax (*see* below). ThermoNatur hemp and jute insulation batts look like good products but it was not possible to get full technical details even though this product is available from an online supplier in Germany.

Detail of cork walls. (Photo: Alex de Rijke)

Hempflax insulation quilt.

Hemp fibre insulation strip, useful for sealing round windows.

Flax and hemp flax fibre blends are also not too common. There is a company called Isolina in Finland, not to be confused with Isolena Sheep Wool in Austria. When contacted, they claimed to have a distributor in the UK called Benkoski, but this is a company that supplies windows. Thermo Hanf is a hemp insulation product produced by the Dutch hemp processing company HempFlax BV, who also have production in Romania.

Hemp Blocks

Isohemp is the main producer of hempcrete blocks in Belgium, owned by HempFlax. HempBuild in Ireland are a distributor but the blocks are shipped from Belgium and they may have other suppliers in the UK. H.G. Matthews in England have been making hemp blocks but it is not clear if these are still available. The Hemp Block Company is a relatively new business, based in Chesham, Buckinghamshire, currently importing hemp blocks from Tecnocanapa-Biodilizia in Italy. The latter company is based near Lake Garda in northern Italy and produces a wide range of hemp lime and other eco products.

Coir/Coconut Fibre

This is mainly used for floor mats and carpeting. First Mats, for instance, produce a range of matting and door mats. Coir boards produced by TNKKSS, a farmers' co-operative in Karnataka in southern India, look like a great product but do not appear to be available in the UK. They also make a coir ply board. There is a huge potential for waste material from coconut and palm oil production to be manufactured into natural building materials in hotter countries, but lack of investment and markets have held this back.

Reed and Clay Boards

Clay boards made by Claytec are a widely used natural alternative to gypsum plasterboard in countries like Germany and Austria. Made in Germany near Düsseldorf and available with ready-made clay plasters, they may be available from UK suppliers like Womersleys and Mike Wye in England. Clay boards could be made in the UK.

Wood Insulation Quilts and Wood Fibre Boards

Wood fibre boards are widely used, manufactured in most European countries but not the UK. One of the leading products, made by Pavatex in Switzerland, involved a wet process, pressing wood waste and using the natural lignins in the wood as a binder. The product had to be dried, though they claimed to use waste wood for the heat as well. Originally manufactured in Cham in Switzerland, Pavatex opened a new facility in Golbey in eastern France. After Pavatex were taken over, the product made in France now may contain additives using a dry process. It is rumoured that the Swiss machinery went to India when the factory in Switzerland was shut down. The new dry process using a glue may not seem to be as ecological but wood fibre is still worth considering as the chemical input is low and the wood fibre boards provide many options. Wood fibre boards are made from wood-processing waste and possibly waste virgin timber. Hundreds of thousands of tonnes of wood waste that could be manufactured into wood fibre boards ends up in landfill in the UK. Pavatex have a range of boards and insulation batts called Pavatherm, Pavadry, Pavaflex and Isolair, and they provide building systems too. Now owned by Soprema, which is mainly involved in synthetic and plastic roofing materials, Pavatex product data sheets show 8 per cent ammonium polyphosphate content, which is claimed to give ninety-minute fire protection.

Gutex is another wood fibre product produced in the German Black Forest near the Swiss border, and is one of the earliest innovators in eco products with Natureplus certification for its products. Its eponymous manufacturers provide a wide range of wood fibre boards and a blown-in wood fibre insulation. These are available through Ecological Building Systems in UK and Ireland, but they may also have other stockists. Gutex contains a polyurethane resin as a binder according to its Health and Safety data sheet but it was not possible to find details of the proportion.

Steicoflex wood fibre board is made by Steico in Germany but there is also a major production facility in Poland. They have a UK base in Luton but distribute through companies such as Ecomerchant. The product may include very small amounts of paraffin, silicate and waterproofing agents but it has not been possible to get full details as the Steico office in England was unwilling to answer questions, simply referring to Ecomerchant. In the same range Steico produce a wood fibre insulation quilt. They have environmental product declarations for some of their products.

Unger Diffutherm, based in Chemnitz near Dresden in Germany, began life in a student flat in 1989 and has grown to a large company trading under the name Udi and manufacturing wood fibre and other insulation boards. Back to Earth was a stockist but no other UK distributor is currently listed.

Beltermo produce a range of wood fibre boards made in Mazyr in Belarus and stocked by Back to Earth in England. There may be problems with this product in the future due to EU sanctions against the Belarus government, and it is suggested that President Lukashenko has been actively involved with the wood-processing industry in that country. (23)

There is the possibility that wood fibre boards might be made in Scotland, as Napier University and Forestry Scotland, at the time of writing, are engaged in research into the potential development

Steico's wood fibre flexible insulation in roof soffit.

of wood fibre manufacturing in Scotland. A report on the potential of wood products in Scotland was produced by Forest Research in Surrey (published in 2012) but failed to consider the potential of wood fibre as an insulation product. (24)

Chipped Wood and Wood Shaving Insulation

Wood shaving insulation is used in some house building but does not seem to be available as a product through merchants. Some academic studies and green building forum discussions have raised doubts about fire safety issues but no evidence of fires in buildings that have used this insulation could be found. Tŷ Unnos in Wales carried out an experimental project with research into wood shavings but do not appear to have developed it any further commercially. (25) A German company, Baufritz, that manufactures prefabricated timber and flat-pack house-building solutions operates in the UK, with a number of UK houses on their website using wood shavings insulation. (26) (27) Baufritz say that they that they follow German Building Biology principles and take account of air quality, 'allergy-compliant construction', intelligent on-demand ventilation, 'electro smog protection' and testing for harmful substances of natural materials and organic insulation. They say that they do not use polyurethane foams, chemical or mineral fibre insulation, toxic adhesives, laminate flooring or solvent-based paints and they claim that they achieve a healthy indoor climate compared with normal UK house builders.

Baufritz state that one of their clients, Andrew Lloyd Webber, only needed one meeting with the Baufritz architect to be convinced of the company's flat-pack concept, having previously had five or six architects design houses that didn't meet his needs when replacing a derelict house on his estate. The Austrian Baubook website states that the Baufritz wall build-up consists of gypsum boards, timber frame and wood chip insulation, a product called Hoiz. The wood chip insulation is treated with whey and soda: the whey is said to be fire-retardant and the soda is said to kill off insects. However, the Baubook certification also says that the wood shavings are coated with silicon and titanium dioxide and some kind of acrylic. (28) Wood shavings could be a useful insulation material as they can be sourced easily, but so far they only seem to be available as part of the Baufritz system.

Magnesium/Calcium Silicate

Calcium silicate boards are often referred to as 'insulation boards' for renovation; they seem to have only limited thermal insulation properties but can be useful for fire protection and they have a breathable lining to reduce mould risks. Some are used more commonly for industrial purposes due to their fire-resistance properties. Products include Calsitherm, made in Paderborn (Germany) and sold as 'climate board'. There are two products, Microcal and Silca: these

Baufritz house, possibly built using wood shavings insulation. (Photo: Baufritz)

can withstand high temperatures but are also able to deal with moisture. Calsitherm has merged with a company called Redstone and the board is being rebranded as **Redboard.** Skamo wall board is a calcium silicate board made by Skamol in Viby (Denmark) who also make a wide range of blocks, boards and other products. Kemwell MultiKem calcium silicate fire protection boards are produced in Birmingham. Promat is another passive fire protection company producing calcium silicate boards. There are a number of silicate boards on the market, some imported from China, which claim to be both moisture-resistant and 'breathable'. Great care should be taken to ensure that when such boards are used with natural insulation materials they provide sufficient vapour permeability.

Natural Materials with Plastic, Chemical and Cement Additives

The materials discussed above are natural materials with limited chemical additions. There is another range of materials which are frequently advertised as natural and healthy but contain a higher level of chemical or synthetic content and need to be considered differently. When discussing this book with a number of architects and specifiers it became apparent that some were either unaware of or were unconcerned about this distinction and thus specified products in the belief that they were natural and chemical-free when in fact they were not. This does not mean that such products should not be considered when selecting products as they may still provide a useful alternative to petrochemical-based insulation materials. The following information about chemical contents has been taken from published manufacturers' health and safety data sheets.

Sheep Wool and Hemp

Thermafleece and Cosywool are well-known brands that pioneered sheep's wool insulation in the UK in

2000. Thermafleece is produced by a company called Eden Renewables Innovations Ltd in Penrith. Their Cosywool product consists of 75 per cent wool, 13 per cent polyester, 10 per cent polyester binder and an unspecified amount of borax salts (presumably 2 per cent by subtraction). (29) The company is based in an old farmhouse but there do not appear to be any manufacturing facilities at their address. Academic research in 2008 said that the products were made by John Cottons in Bradford, though production may well be carried out elsewhere. (30)

Tŷ-Mawr say that their Welsh Cosywool product is made from wool sourced in Wales but this seems to be the same Thermafleece product described above. Normally wool used for industrial production is sourced through British Wool (previously known as the Wool Marketing Board). This means it is hard to say where the wool has come from but maybe they have found a way round this to obtain wool from Welsh farmers. Eden Renewables also produce something called Thermafleece NatraHemp, which contains 20 per cent polyester and 10 per cent polyester binder plus 10 per cent ammonium polyphosphate. They also produce SupaSoft Insulation, which is made from recycled plastic bottles, using 85 per cent polyester and 15 per cent unspecified binder (glue). It was not possible to find out what flame-retardant chemicals are used in SupaSoft.

Black Mountain Insulation was set up in Rhyl in North Wales with the support of the Welsh government but has subsequently been taken over, following a fire in the factory, and it is not clear whether the manufacturing still takes place in Wales. They also advertise Natuwool and NatraHemp. It was not possible to find a COSHH Health and Safety data sheet, which is legally required to display the chemical constituents, but a data sheet refers to 95 per cent natural fibre with 5 per cent 'combination recycled adhesive binder'.

Given the fact that there are about 15 million sheep in the UK and farmers get paid very little for the fleeces, it seems ridiculous that there is not more production of sheep's wool insulation in the UK and

Sheep's wool insulation containing polyester binder.

Woodwool boards.

Ireland. The price of wool has fallen significantly in recent years and apparently much of it is either composted or goes to landfill. While there has been occasional negative publicity about moth infestations, wool is naturally fire retardant, is claimed to absorb chemicals such as formaldehyde and is also able to help with humidity regulation. There are stories about houses being built using untreated fleeces direct from sheep as insulation; this is not advisable as the wool contains many bugs and needs scouring and cleaning and the wool may have been treated with organophosphates.

Woodwool

Woodwool boards are useful products in eco construction and can provide some acoustic insulation and a good breathable base for plastering and hempcrete. Woodwool was made in Europe for many years with a magnesium carbonate binder and there are still products made this way in India. However, the industry in Europe has changed to using cement, which means the product is viewed by some as less sustainable. The boards are also considerably heavier than the previous magnesium carbonate boards. Heraklith is a board made from wood chips and magnesium carbonate that was much used in eco building but the company was acquired by Knauf who may have changed the production methods. An environmental

product declaration (EPD) refers to the use of a mineral binding agent, magnesite and cement. Savolit boards are mainly sold as acoustic panels and are made (by Troldtekt in Denmark) from mineralized wood chips with cement as the bonding agent. There are a range of products including an external insulation board called Savotherm, but made with mineral wool, not natural insulation. Celenit boards are made in Italy; its producers claim their huge range of boards are natural and useful as part of thermal and acoustic insulation. They provide some of the most extensive range of technical data sheets for any product referred to here. The boards are made from mineralized fir wood, Portland cement and marble dust. The last is a much under-used waste mineral resource that is available in large quantities, particularly in Italy but also Portugal, and could be included as a cementitious binder in some natural products.

'Natural' Materials from Recycled Resources with Some Chemical Input

Recycled Glass, Clay and Perlite Aggregates

Foamglas manufacture and supply cellular glass insulation in the form of a wide range of blocks and boards available through mainstream UK builders' merchants. Foamglas have a wide range of certifications including from Natureplus. The products are largely made from recycled glass with some additives and have many useful properties, including being impermeable to water and non-flammable, and they can be used on roofs and underground and in sub-floors where few other eco materials can be used, an ideal replacement for polystyrene. It is to be hoped that if this material were more widely used its cost might come down as it is currently much more expensive than polystyrene. Geocell make a wide range of glass products including foam glass bubbles consisting of 70 per cent glass plus other chemicals including sodium, calcium, aluminium, magnesium and potassium oxides. Made in Germany, Austria and Switzerland, they produce a glass gravel for foundations and backfill where breathability is required. This is widely used for limecrete and hempcrete floors but can be used on roofs and in many other situations. Technopor is another foamed glass product for use in floors, made by Dreieck near Vienna in Austria. They also make expanded clay aggregates but it was not possible to find a UK distributor at the time of writing.

Made by Plasmor in Yorkshire, TechniClay is a lightweight expanded clay aggregate suitable for limecrete floors; it is made by expanding clay to five times its volume in a kiln. The finished product is widely available from a range of UK merchants. Plasmor also make building blocks which appear to blend their lightweight clay aggregate with cement. Leca make expanded clay balls which can provide a similar solution but at the time of writing its website was not available. Expanded perlite can also be used as insulation. Perlite is a form of volcanic glass which is mined and then heated to expand to eighty times its natural volume; it is used to provide an insulated lining to chimney flues and is available from many builders' merchants.

Cotton and Other Fabric Waste

The Inno-Therm product featured in my 2006 *Natural Building* book is still in production. Owned by Recovery Insulation Ltd of Sheffield, this quilt insulation is made from recycled denim by Métisse Insulation in France. It is a mix of recycled textiles, cotton (70 per cent), acrylic fibres and wool, and includes 15 per cent polyester with added fungicide. It was not possible to discover what flame retardant is used but it is likely to be borax. It has a poor published fire rating (F) but reasonable insulation performance and would normally be used enclosed in fire-retardant products like gypsum boards. Given the large quantities of waste clothing available and the fact that 20 per cent of landfill is said to consist of discarded clothes, surely much more could be done with this waste resource. While much of this is from synthetic material, heavily dosed with hazardous flame retardants, it should still be possible to separate natural wool and cotton products and this could be used to make insulation.

Flax Insulation Quilts

Various flax insulation products are made in Europe but suppliers in the UK could not be found or indeed details of chemical constituents, though most appear to contain synthetic binders. Isovlas is a Dutch insulation made from flax in two forms, PL and PN, but did not seem to be available in the UK at the time of writing.

Recycled cotton insulation (Photo: Métisse)

Mushroom or Fungus Insulation

Research has been undertaken for a number of years to create insulation and building materials from mushrooms and fungus. This seems to be a very exciting idea and there is talk of factory production beginning in the near future. This seems some way off achieving commercial availability in the UK, though Biohm seems well established (31) and there is another company called Greensulate in the US.

Cellulose – Recycled Paper Insulation

Cellulose insulation is possibly mis-named. Cellulose is a complex carbohydrate in the walls of plant material and not really an accurate term for recycled waste paper, but this insulation product has been referred to as cellulose for many years. Recycled paper insulation has been regarded as a 'natural' eco material and is the first choice for many architects designing sustainable buildings. In order to cope with issues of fire safety and rot and damp risks, this product is dosed with borax although some companies have tried to reduce this through the addition of magnesium sulphate. Borax salts and boric acid are chemicals considered by some to be hazardous, with the vast majority mined by global multinational Rio Tinto, and

Mycelium fungus insulation. (Photo: Biohm)

there were plans in the EU to ban its use and put it on the risk register, which industry successfully resisted. The dust from borax can cause irritation to skin and particularly the eyes and so protective gear should be used when borax-treated products are being installed.

Recycled paper insulation can be installed by self-builders but is normally sprayed by specialist installers into timber frame build-ups which often include plastic airtightness membranes. There were problems with the insulation slumping in cavities in the early days, which manufacturers say is no longer a problem as there is now greater adhesion in the mix. The thermal performance of recycled cellulose is sometimes exaggerated, but a lambda value of 0.38 is generally accepted, which is adequate to meet current building regulations.

Given the popularity of recycled waste paper insulation it is likely to remain in widespread use, despite questions about the chemical content. It has been reported that homeowners have complained about smells from ammonium sulphate after installation, and others argue that there can be off-gassing from the fire-retardant chemicals, insecticides, solvents and inks from the original paper waste. However, toxicity studies remain inconclusive. When other natural materials with negligible chemical content are available, as featured in this book, it is hard to know why a product dependent on chemicals is so popular, but many architects seem happy to accept the use of borax despite questions about the health effects of borate-based emissions. (32)

Warmcel is a widely used product in the UK. It was produced in South Wales by Excel Industries, a 38-year-old company which closed in 2014 with press reports stating that a new smaller factory would open. In fact, production was shifted to CIUR in the Czech Republic. CIUR declare the following constituents: cellulose pulp >80 per cent, boric acid <5.5 per cent, magnesium sulphate 5–15 per cent. CIUR have an office in Aberdare in South Wales but work through their distributor PYC in mid-Wales, who act as the main agent for CIUR. There are local specialist installers for Warmcel in most parts of the UK and a few in Ireland.

Thermofloc is a 'cellulose' insulation made in Austria. Thermofloc F is claimed to be borate-free whereas Thermofloc B is a reduced borate product. These products have Natureplus certification with a stated fire rating of E, but B when a calcium silicate board is used. It is available from some UK merchants, with Ecomerchant claiming on their website that it is cheaper than Warmcel. It is supplied in bags and can be spread by hand in lofts without a specialist installer but can also be blown into cavities if a specialist installer can be found. Ecocel is manufactured in Cork in Ireland by Cellulose Insulation Ltd from what they describe on their data sheet as 'wood-based' cellulose fibre (80 per cent) but recycled newspapers are also mentioned. Treated with magnesium hydroxide (6 per cent) and boric acid (>5.5 per cent), it also includes calcium sulphate and calcium carbonate.

Recycled Glass Fibre and Other Sources

Knauf Earthwool is not a natural product, strictly speaking, but as glass fibre has been the most widely used and cheapest insulation for many years it is important to discuss it as the industry started to refer to 'mineral fibre' a few years ago after glass fibre had acquired such a bad name. Mineral fibre is sometimes referred to as a natural material.

Glass fibre insulation was categorized as carcinogenic in the US but the Environmental Protection Agency was forced to withdraw this classification in 2001, after substantial legal action by the industry. This remains a controversial issue. Some mineral fibre insulations contain significant levels of formaldehyde which is listed by the World Health Organization as carcinogenic. Some products are now described as formaldehyde- (and phenol-) free but, in reality, this means that no formaldehyde has been added, a subtle difference. Glass fibre was unpopular with builders as it was itchy and caused allergic reactions. If you have pink or yellow glass fibre in your loft (though after a few years it will look grey and dirty) you may want to remove it and replace it with a natural insulation. It

is important to take great care when disturbing this material when working in a loft or when removing it as the fibres are tiny and can get into every corner of your house. It is important to ensure that the loft hatch is well sealed to stop stray fibres getting into the house as some people can have allergic reactions and you don't want your children breathing in the fibres.

Knauf began to produce a new mineral fibre insulation using what they called 'ECOSE' technology and rebranded it with the name 'Earthwool' which may sound to some like a natural product, claiming to use natural raw materials 'that are rapidly renewable' with no added formaldehyde or phenols, and using a 'bio-based' binder. The glass fibre insulation is made from 'man-made vitreous silicate fibres' with alkaline oxide and alkaline 'earth' oxide. They use a polymer plant-based bonding agent (glue) which is sometimes referred to as a natural resin. As most of these constituents are 'commercially confidential' you will need to come to your own conclusions about whether these insulation products are acceptable for those want to build with natural materials.

Stone wool is another mineral fibre product, made from melted stone and sometimes described as a natural material as the original source is from natural stone. However, the high level of energy used and the number of chemicals involved do not fall within the definition of 'natural' in this book. It is possible that power station waste and blast furnace slag may be used in some mineral wool insulations but information on this was hard to find. Stone wool products are widely used due to their claimed fire resistance and are now being extensively used instead of plastic foam insulations following the Grenfell disaster. A major campaign against the opening of a new Rockwool factory in Virginia in the US has led to the publication of data on expected emissions from the factory chimney. (33)

There is no doubt that the above list of products is not complete. New ones will emerge in the next year or two, but I have tried to make this as comprehensive as possible to give people who want to build a natural home as many options as possible.

Suppliers, Materials And Products

Please do not assume that any of the companies or products listed here are endorsed by the author; 'buyer beware' still applies. No money (or even discounts) has been accepted from any suppliers listed here so it is up to the readers to make their own checks. Information is correct at the time of writing but may have changed before the book went to press.

Suppliers

Acara Concepts (Ireland and UK), https://www.acaraconcepts.com/

Back to Earth (Devon), https://www.backtoearth.co.uk/

Best of Lime (Suffolk), https://bestoflime.co.uk/

Celtic Sustainables (Ceredigion), https://www.celticsustainables.co.uk/

Ecomerchant (UK), https://www.ecomerchant.co.uk/

Ecological Building Systems (Cumbria and Ireland), https://www.ecologicalbuildingsystems.com/

Heritage Ltd (Co. Antrim, Northern Ireland), https://www.heritageltd.com/

Lime Green (Shropshire), https://www.lime-green.co.uk/

Masons Mortar (Edinburgh), https://masonsmortar.co.uk/

Mike Wye (Devon), https://www.mikewye.co.uk/

North Woods Design (Ross-shire), https://www.northwoodsdesign.co.uk

Roundtower (Co. Cork, Ireland), https://www.roundtowerlime.com/

Scottish Lime Centre Trust (Fifeshire), https://www.scotlime.org/

Sheep Wool Insulation (Co. Wicklow, Ireland), https://www.sheepwoolinsulation.com/

Stoneware Studios (Co. Cork, Ireland), http://www.stonewarestudios.com/

Tŷ-Mawr (Powys), https://www.lime.org.uk/

Unity Lime (Yorkshire), https://unitylime.co.uk/

Womersleys (Yorkshire), https://www.womersleys.co.uk/

Materials and Products

Amorim (Portugal), https://www.amorimcorkinsulation.com/en/products/

Beltermo (Belarus), https://beltermo.com/

Biohm Ltd (London), https://www.biohm.co.uk/

Bioizol (Czech Republic), https://www.bioizol.eu/en/hemp-insulation-panel

Bioizol (Czech Republic), https://www.bioizol.eu/en/hemp-insulation-bio-flex

Black Mountain (Essex), https://www.blackmountaininsulation.com/NatuWool_Technical_Sheet.pdf

Celenit (Italy), https://www.celenit.com/en-UK/concept-building-construction.php

Claytec (Germany), https://www.claytec.de/en/products/clay-drybuilding/clayboard-d20-d25_pid205

Diasen Diathonite (Italy), https://www.diasen.com/en/thermal-and-acoustic-insulation/

Duprée Minerals Ltd (Staffordshire), https://www.dupreminerals.com/perlite

First Mats (Birmingham), https://www.firstmats.co.uk/blogs/buying-guides/what-is-coir-matting

Foamglas (London), https://www.foamglas.com/en-gb/products/

Geocell (Germany), www.geocell-schaumglas.eu

Gutex (Germany), https://gutex.co.uk/home/

H. G. Matthews Ltd (Buckinghamshire), https://www.hgmatthews.com/lime-and-cob/natural-building-blocks/hempcrete-blocks/

Hemp Block (Buckinghamshire), https://hempblock.co.uk/

Hemp Build (Co. Meath, Ireland), https://www.hempbuild.ie/shop/hempflaxplus

Hemp Flax (The Netherlands), https://www.hempflax.com/en/applications/construction/hemp-insulation/

Inno-Therm (Sheffield), http://www.inno-therm.com/

Isolena (Austria), https://www.lehner-wool.com/en/isolena/

Isolina (Finland), http://www.isolina.com/gb/insulation-contact.cfm

Isovlas (The Netherlands), https://www.isovlas.nl/bouwisolatie/

Kemwell (Birmingham), https://www.kemwell-fire.com/passive-fire-protection-boards/multikem-mp1000-calcium-silicate-board/

Knauf Heraklith (worldwide), http://closetheloop.gr/edss/wp-content/uploads/2015/03/Knauf-Insulation-EPD-Heraklith-35-mm-example.pdf

Leca (Chester), https://www.leca.co.uk

Métisse (France), https://materialdistrict.com/material/metisse-recycled-textile-insulation/

Pavatex (Switzerland and worldwide), https://www.pavatex.com/en/company/company-portrait/

Plasmor (Yorkshire), https://www.plasmor.co.uk/products-services/techniclay-aggregate

Promat (Bristol), https://www.promat.co.uk/en-gb/products

Savolit Skanda (Wrexham, N. Wales), https://www.savolit.co.uk/

Secil (Portugal), https://www.secil-group.com/a-secil/a-secil-no-mundo/a-secil-no-mundo-portugal/?lang=en

Silca (Germany), www.silca-online.de

Skamol (Denmark), www.skamol.com

Soprema (France), https://www.soprema.co.uk/en/gamme/insulation/pavatex

Steico (Germany), https://www.steico.com/en/products/wood-fibre-insulation/steicoflex/overview/ and

Tecnocampa (Italy), https://tecnocanapa-bioedilizia.it/

Thermafleece (Cumbria), https://www.thermafleece.com/product/thermafleece-cosywool-sheep-s-wool-flexible-slab

Thermo Natur (Germany), https://www.naturanum.de/thermo-natur/

Thermofloc (Germany), https://www.thermofloc.com/contacts/germany

TNKKSS (India), https://www.tnkkss.org/coco-peat-blocks

Troldtekt (Denmark), https://www.troldtekt.com/

Unger Diffutherm (Germany), https://www.udidaemmsysteme.com/udi-system/for-the-facade/udireco-system/

Warmcel and PYC (Powys), https://www.warmcel.co.uk/about/distribution/

References

1. Tom Woolley, *Natural Building: A Guide to Materials and Techniques* (The Crowood Press, 2006).
2. https://companycheck.co.uk/
3. https://companycheck.co.uk/company/08714419/BLACK-MOUNTAIN-INSULATION-LIMITED/companies-house-data
4. https://companycheck.co.uk/company/04486900/INTERNATIONAL-PETROLEUM-PRODUCTS-LIMITED/companies-house-data
5. https://www.intpetro.com/building-products-range/
6. https://www.soprema.co.uk/en/gamme/insulation/pavatex
7. https://www.kingfisher.com/en/media/news/kingfisher-news/2021/kingfisher-announces-new-planet-and-community-responsible-busine.html
8. https://www.theguardian.com/uk-news/2020/nov/26/celotex-executive-wrote-wtf-on-fire-test-report-grenfell-inquiry-hears
9. Tom Woolley, *Low Impact Building: Housing Using Renewable Materials* (Wiley, 2013).
10. https://www.cmostores.com/about-insulation-superstore/
11. https://www.biofib.com/

12. https://www.cavac-biomateriaux.com/
13. https://www.ecomerchant.co.uk/
14. https://www.gov.uk/tax-on-shopping/energy-saving-products#:~:text=Energy%20products%20that%20qualify,walls%2C%20floors%2C%20ceilings%20and%20lofts)
15. https://www.bbacerts.co.uk/
16. https://www.kiwa.com/gb/en/products/construction-materials-testing/
17. https://www.natureplus.org/index.php?id=1&L=2
18. https://www.labc.co.uk/labc-assured
19. https://www.labss.org/national-approvals/abc-assured-rd-search
20. https://www.bregroup.com/greenguide/podpage.jsp?id=2126
21. http://larenaissance.org.uk/
22. Oliver Wilton and Matthew Barnett Howland, 'Cork Construction Kit', *The Journal of Architecture*, 2020, 25:2, 138–165.
23. https://www.belarus.by/en/business/business-news/lukashenko-urges-to-develop-wood-production_i_0000119628.html
24. https://forestry.gov.scot/publications/625-scottish-government-biomass-incentives-review-best-use-of-wood-fibre-report)
25. http://www.tyunnos.co.uk/wp-content/uploads/2016/04/insulation-from-wood-shavings.pdf
26. https://buildingbiology.com/blown-in-wood-chip-insulation/
27. https://www.baufritz.com/uk/contact-and-catalogue/news/1867-andrew-lloyd-webber-has-built-with-baufritz/#read
28. https://www.baubook.at/m/PHP/Info.php?SI=2142723907&SW=32&win=y
29. https://www.thermafleece.com/product/thermafleece-cosywool-sheep-s-wool-flexible-slab
30. https://www.researchgate.net/figure/Flow-Chart-of-Thermafleece-Secondary-Processing-at-John-Cotton-Manufacturing_fig2_237471858
31. https://www.biohm.co.uk/mycelium
32. https://www.webmd.com/a-to-z-guides/borax-sodium-tetraborate
33. Daniel L. Morgan, *NTP Toxicity Study Report on the Atmospheric Characterization, Particle Size, Chemical Composition, and Workplace Exposure Assessment of Cellulose Insulation (CELLULOSEINS)*, US National Toxicology Programme Toxicity Report Series 74, August 2006

Chapter Eight

PAINTS AND FINISHES

Colours and attractive internal finishes can make a huge difference to the experience of living in a building. While internal finishes are very much a matter of personal choice and something that the occupants may have more control over, if you have constructed or renovated a building using natural materials it is essential to finish it off with appropriate materials. If you have vapour-permeable (breathable) walls it is important to use breathable paints rather than sealing them up with plastic finishes. When mainstream builders started using hempcrete, they continued to use impermeable plasters and plastic paints, which then trapped moisture in the walls. (1) This wrongly gave a bad reputation to hempcrete as not drying out, when the problem was caused partially by the finishes, not the hempcrete.

Natural finishes should be good for your health as they will contribute to reducing emissions in buildings. Plenty are available though they may not always be as easy to obtain as conventional paints and finishes. There is a great deal of misinformation and confusion about paints and a lack of standards and definition of what constitutes a natural paint. Cost may be a factor and there are some very cheap paints available, but these should be avoided when there are plenty of excellent natural products and materials. First of all it is important to understand what is wrong with conventional paints.

Hazardous Paints

Toxic emissions from paints and paint strippers were of great concern in the 1970s and changes were brought in through various EU regulations that led to significant reductions in volatile organic compound (VOC) emissions in particular. These emissions, which were mainly from the solvents used in paints, were to be declared on the tin. The aim was to encourage the industry to produce low VOC paints. (2) This regulation was taken up by UK paint companies but it is not always easy to find the information. Some companies have adopted a labelling system which is published in some guides, (3) but this is not officially required. As a result, many paints are now marketed as VOC-free or low VOC, which may give the impression that they are now healthy or even natural. However, paints contain a wide range of synthetic chemicals such as fungicides, antimicrobials and preservatives which are there to ensure longevity in the containers, and these can also be of health concern. Do not take the 'low VOC' label as an indication that the paint is environmentally friendly. There are also many paints and varnishes still available which are high in VOC emissions and there is no doubt that there is a market for the more toxic products as some people believe that they are better than low VOC products.

Solvents such as white spirit are still available and are used to dilute certain paints and to clean brushes. Paint strippers, such as methylene chloride, are used widely and can be highly toxic, though ecological paint strippers are also available. When carrying out indoor air quality sampling to identify emissions from materials and other sources it is normal to remove stored paints and decorating products from the building as well as cleaning materials as these can cause significant emissions which can mask other toxic chemicals. If you are concerned

this does not mean that these products are environmentally friendly.

Paint companies are particularly difficult in that some do not publish health and safety data sheets, sometimes stating that they are available on request. Requesting such data sheets has proved to be a difficult exercise when preparing this book. While many construction materials companies have signed up to a range of ecological certification schemes, the paint companies, even some of the leading eco paint manufacturers, have failed to do this. There is no evidence that paint manufacture is any more competitive than the production of other materials, such as insulation, and yet the chemicals and metals used in paints are seen as highly commercially confidential.

A serious health concern is the use of biocides as preservatives in paint containers and tins, such as 5-chloro-2-methyl-(2H)-isothiazol-3-one, 2-methyl-2(H)-isothiazol-3-one, 1,2-benzisothiazol-3(2H)-one and Bronopol. These may even be used with more natural low-emission paints. Recent research has revealed the widespread use of PFAs in paints and coatings as consumer demand has risen for dirtproof, washable and so-called self-cleaning paints: PFAs are per- and poly-fluoroalkyl chemicals, which were developed for use in products like non-stick pans. Campaigns against the pollution caused by the manufacture of these chemicals were highlighted by the book *Exposure* (4) and the film *Dark Waters* (5). It has become clear that PFAs are polluting chemicals in

about health it's worth having a purge on all the old tins and bottles from decorating that can pile up in a cupboard, and either get them safely disposed of or recycled, or at least stored in an outside shed. It's also worth remembering that these products also represent a serious fire risk.

One particular paint company has been hugely successful in recent years and is often referred to as being environmentally friendly, as it has specialized in reproducing traditional colours. For legal reasons, it is not possible to refer to this company by name but it offers a range of conventional paints, and also 'natural' paints such as casein, distemper and limewash, but the blood of many people, as persistent pollutants of serious health concern. It has been suggested that they are being used more and more in paints and coatings. (6)

Standard Paints

Conventional emulsion paints are usually water-based. They are composed of pigments, binders, acrylic polymers (plastics) and a carrier which is usually water. Micro plastic and synthetic micro fibres are increasingly used in paints and may be contributing to pollution of watercourses and the oceans. (7) (8) Colour pigments used may include cadmium, cobalt, manganese, chromium and even lead, even though lead paints were banned in 1978.

Newspapers have reported that some people become sick from the fumes from water-based emulsion paints, and there are still VOC emissions from low VOC paints; some people can be allergic or hypersensitive to the chemicals used. Pregnant woman and babies should not be exposed to fresh paints of any kind, even for some months before and after the birth, so don't be tempted to redecorate the nursery for the new baby!

Oil-based paints, gloss and eggshell can be much higher odour and release higher levels of chemical VOC pollutants from solvents. Similar problems exist with varnishes and wood oils. It is necessary to be very cautious when buying paints and not believe everything that it says on the tin! Sadly, some products advertised as eco paints are not as ecological as you might hope. A good guide is when companies do not provide easy access to health and safety data sheets. In contrast, some of the best eco paint companies do this so you can find the data with one click on their website. If the health and safety data sheets are hidden then you know there is something to hide.

Natural Paints

Biofa (9) emerged in Germany in the 1970s, followed by Auro (10) and Livos (11) in 1983. These companies have pioneered natural paints and they have survived and become commercially successful. They claim their paints are plant-based and largely chemical-free. You can easily access their health and safety data sheets from their websites, which show constituents such as natural turpentine and orange oil. Natural oils are, of course, chemicals of sorts and they do point out that these paints should not be disposed of into the sewage system. They give a great deal of information on other raw materials they use which may include dammar resin, plant resin soap, lime and many hundreds of other natural materials. Chemicals include potassium sorbate, balsamic turpentine, quartz sand and salt, and possibly titanium dioxide (for white paints) is used as there is such a high demand for sparkling white walls. A wide range of colours are available.

Auro wood stain (apologies to Auro for this old tin but the paint keeps very well).

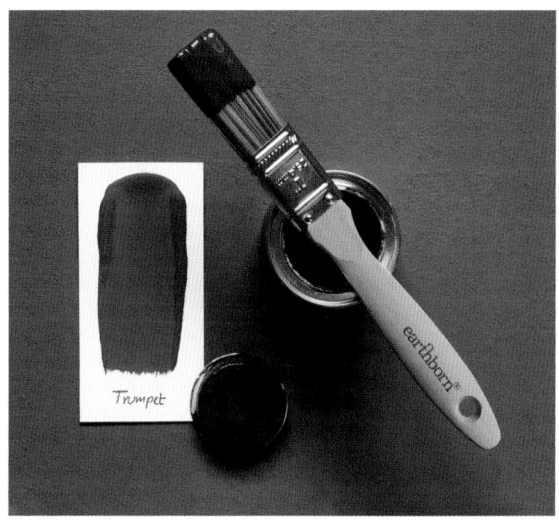

Clay paint from Earthborn. (Photo: Earthborn Paints)

Biofa also have a strong focus on wood treatments and oils as well as general paints; they work with a UK importer called GreenSteps. (12)

Livos have a wide range of products including internal and external wood paints, internal decorative paints and a range of plasters and other useful treatments, including mould remover and cleaning materials. They even make a range of products for horses like hoof balm and saddle soap. Livos products are available from several UK distributors. (13) They also say they own their own linseed oil press.

Osmo (14) are based in Germany, but their wood oil and stain products have become widely used by the UK flooring industry once workpeople realized that they didn't get sick like they did from the solvents in conventional products. As a result, Osmo is widely available in conventional high street paint stores. Many of their products may not be as natural and chemical-free as Auro, Biofa and Livos, so a random search of their many safety data sheets (also very easy to find) reveal the use of aliphatic hydrocarbons, dipropylene glycol, monomethyl ether and propiconazole in their 'natural' oil wood stain and they are open that their products contain some solvents. Their combination of natural oils and chemicals does offer a range of products which provide good weather resistance and longevity when used on external timber.

Osmo uses carefully harvested natural oils (sunflower, soya, linseed and thistle) and hard waxes (carnauba and candelilla) for its finishes. The inorganic pigments used for Osmo wood finishes are created from natural ores; these

Timber cladding and timber window painted with natural oil-based wood stains – in good condition after fifteen years of driving rain.

Timber cladding stained with Osmo.

Osmo wood oil.

are cleaned and refined until a level of physiological purity has been achieved and only a pure mineral element remains. Osmo has been working for many years with 'High Solid Products' which contain only a small amount of solvents. (15)

Earthborn Paints (16) may appear to be a UK product from its website, with its main office in Cheshire owned by Gordon Products Ltd. Like Osmo, its products are widely available in the UK but are probably manufactured in Germany by Ecotech Naturfarben in Ludenscheid. The Earthborn products are clay paints but there are also other Ecotec and Volvox (17) products. Their range extends into emulsions, eggshell and Ecopro silicate masonry paints.

Anyone who has experienced applying clay paints will find it hard to go back to conventional acrylic emulsions as they are creamy and easy to apply, often only requiring one coat depending on what surface it is being applied to.

Earthborn claim to be the first paint company to embrace EU eco labelling which is available through Ecotec Naturfarben. (18) Their safety data sheets weren't quite as easy to find but they are there. It was necessary to go to a stockists' website to find the data sheet for clay paint which reveals that it contains 2-methyl-2H-isothiazol-3-one and 1,2-benzisothiazol-3(2H)-one, though only in very small concentrations. (19)

Earthborn are frank about the need to use some preservatives but once you have tried clay paints you are unlikely to worry about these. Auro also make a clay paint and Livos do a 'clay-containing' paint.

Clay paint.
(Photo: Earthborn Paints)

'Natural' is often used as shorthand for 'healthy, wholesome and eco'. However, many traditional natural ingredients in paint can also be hazardous. Think about lead and turpentine (derived from trees) which are either banned or controlled because of the harmful effect on health and the environment. When people ask for 'natural' they usually mean healthy and eco-friendly, and those are the criteria we use at Earthborn when formulating our paints.

We would advise to be suspicious of any paint claiming to be a natural paint as there is no such thing as a liquid natural paint

Clay paint applied to lime-plastered hempcrete wall.

in a tin. All paints by necessity contain some synthetic chemicals (for instance, water-based paints require a preservative to keep them 'fresh'). (20)

Casein Paints

Casein paints are made from milk and are sometimes referred to as distemper. They have been in use since ancient times and you can produce your own casein paints at home. Many famous artists would have used casein paints as a base for their artwork. Manufacturing casein paints usually involves lime but sometimes ammonium carbonate or borax is used. Casein is precipitated from milk with the use of rennet and then pigments are added. Casein powder is available from some paint suppliers like Earthborn and various art suppliers, sometimes described as 'milk paint'. If you want to make it at home you need to leave milk in a warm place for a few days to curdle. You then strain it through cheesecloth, leaving the curds which are then mixed with lime. Water can be added once it is blended, and crushed coloured pigments can be added. Various fillers can be added. There are casein paints and casein and lime fillers available from commercial natural paint companies. (21)

Vegan Paints

Some companies offer 'natural paints' that they say are suitable for vegans as no animals were harmed in their manufacture. Generally, paint products do not involve animal products anyway, so most natural paints can be considered suitable for vegans and this may be seen more as a clever marketing device. Vegans, however, may want to avoid one of the most natural paints made from casein as they may regard the production of milk as cruel. At least one brand of vegan paints includes graphene as a constituent (*see* below).

Feng Shui Paints

Adherents of feng shui may be able to explain this, but again this looks more like clever marketing than a serious alternative form of paint. Feng shui paints are described as giving a harmonious feel to a home, suffusing light gently, but you may be able to achieve this with other natural paints of course.

Air-Purifying Paints

There are a handful of companies offering a range of materials and paint products that claim to purify air. As householders become more aware of the pollution coming into the house from outdoor traffic and industrial and agricultural pollution, as well as emissions from VOCs in the home, the idea of air-purifying paints will seem attractive. *Do not be fooled.* Having investigated several air-purifying paint products it becomes clear that there is little evidence that they are able to absorb toxic particles and chemicals. Test reports on these products confirm that they are biocidal and anti-bacterial, and this will reduce the risk of microbes forming on the surfaces. However, most paints today contain fungicides and other chemicals to try and mitigate bacterial and mould problems, so the so-called air-purifying paints (some of which are extremely expensive) may not be adding anything new. The fungicide and other active chemicals may in fact be making the paints less healthy!

Some claim that purifying paints reduce NO_2 particulates. NO_2 particulates are a serious product of traffic pollution but there may be other materials which are more effective at mitigating air pollution. Some companies selling such paints simply claim that they are the only VOC-free product available, but this is simply reducing emissions, which can indeed be seen as purifying the air. There are also claims of using a molecular sieve or silicate air filter to absorb the air-borne pollutants. Independent evaluation of the effectiveness of this could not be found.

Graphene Paints

Some companies that claim to sell natural paints offer a range that includes graphene in the formulation. They claim that the 'natural' graphene fibres give properties such as improved thermal conductivity, greater toughness, strength, flexibility and uniformity, describing it as 'pure inert carbon-based technology'. Graphene is made from carbon and you can make it yourself at home by mixing graphite with water and washing-up liquid! It appears that graphene is used in paints as nano-particles which act as a mesh at the molecular level; this is claimed to create a greater durability through lower maintenance. Graphene is said to be stronger than structural steel, allowing the paint to flex by up to 20 per cent. It is added to some natural paint and lime formulations using a graphene polymer. There have been serious concerns about nano-particles being carcinogenic and this is subject to scientific investigation, though the graphene paint products are claimed not to be bio-persistent. If you are excited by new nano-technology you might want to try these products but others might prefer to apply the precautionary principle. There are numerous scientific papers raising concerns about toxicity problems related to graphene.

Wood Stains

Wood stains can be made from a range of natural oils; they penetrate the wood rather than coating it. Many wood oils are low in VOCs today and so are much easier to use without having to leave all the windows open for days. External wood stains may contain some solvents but can be much more effective than traditional gloss paints. Gloss paints deteriorate in UV light and weathering and so repainting is necessary every three or four years. Good wood stains should last much longer and if they contain some solvents, when used outside this is less of a health problem. Wood oils and varnishes can be made with natural oils such as linseed oil but this can still be regarded as a VOC. Natural oil-based varnishes with added minerals were available for a time to protect external timber from UV light, but these ran into problems with EU VOC emissions limits and are not available any more.

Paint Stripping

Stripping old paint can be a dangerous activity. In an old house, you may be trying to remove lead paint and burning it off or sanding it off can release toxic chemicals into the home. Solvent-based paint strippers are extremely dangerous and should be avoided. Some contain methylene chloride which is suspected of being carcinogenic, and the fumes have even led to deaths. However, there are a wide range of water-based paint strippers, some of which are made by natural paint companies already referred to, but there are other products such as Home Strip, Smart Strip and Biostrip and many more. Products can be made of soy gel, citrus and baking soda. It is always best to try out such products in the open air on a small sample to make sure you are happy to use the product; wear gloves and wash your hands frequently. (22)

Some products are advertised as suitable to remove Artex, which was a fibrous plaster used to make ceilings and walls lumpy or swirly. Some fibrous plasters may have been made with asbestos prior to 1970s so you should take great care and arrange for a sample to be tested before trying to remove it. There are numerous websites advocating ways of dealing with rough fibrous plaster, either by plastering over or covering with plasterboard. ('Artex' is often used as a generic term but there is a company called Artex which appears to be part of Saint Gobain Ltd and no criticism of this company is intended here.)

Silicate External Paints

Mineral silicate paints are made from potash water glass with lime, quartz-based fillers and mineral pigments. The lime-based silicate paints absorb carbon dioxide much like lime used in mortars and renders. They are designed to be much more weather-resistant than traditional limewashing or lime paints. The best known product is Keim. Mr Keim invented silicate paints in the 1870s and they have proved to be very successful when used on lime-based masonry surfaces, helping to maintain the breathability of the fabric. (23) A useful account of the history and nature of silicate paints can be found on Womersley's website. (24). Another German mineral paint is produced by Beeck. (25)

Several of the natural paint companies listed above offer a range of silicate paints and so do some of the lime companies like Secil. There are also ethyl silicates and zinc silicates. It is important not to confuse silicate paints with *silicone*, so-called waterproof paints, and masonry coatings. These waterproofing treatments are not necessarily breathable and may prevent your lime-based wall from dealing with moisture. Designed to keep water out, they can also trap water in the walls! Most silicone masonry paints are likely to be made from petrochemicals.

Wallpaper, Cork and Wood Linings

It is rare to decorate houses with wallpaper today and great care should be taken not to use adhesives contaminated with high levels of fungicide and other hazardous chemicals.

There are many wallpaper products branded as 'natural' but this generally refers to the use of leaves and plants in the decorative design, rather than the materials used. It is even possible to find vinyl (plastic) wallpaper advertised as natural. Even 'organic' wallpaper and fabrics refer to the plant-based designs, not the materials. It took quite a bit of searching to find lining material using pure natural compostable materials and they do exist, but none provided any technical back-up to support their claims. Products

are made from flax fibres and viscose, made from wood fibre.

Isolena, whose sheep's wool insulation is featured elsewhere, offer chemical-free woollen felt materials for wall linings, a product called Silentum, which also serves as an acoustic sound-dampening material. (26)

Cork is sometimes used as a wall finish. It is mounted onto a backing material which can be glued to walls, with a wide range of colours and decorative effects. It proved difficult to find out what glues would normally be used and whether the cork is coated with synthetic materials and colours. These can generally be rather overdesigned and a very expensive product, but it is worth checking out a range of cork wallpapers, rolls and decorative panels from Amorim. (27)

Recycled Paints

Vast quantities of paint get wasted. Garages and sheds throughout the land are cluttered with half-full tins of unused paint. Other tins get thrown into landfill, creating a serious pollution problem. There are schemes and organizations to recycle paint, however, and using recycled paints might appeal to some who want to reduce waste. There are schemes around the world: Resene Paint in New Zealand; Paintback in Australia; Paintcare in the US; Paint Care Association in Canada; Paintcare, New Life Paints, Seagulls, Community Repaint and Paint 360 in the UK and Rediscover Paint in Ireland. Most public recycling centres now include containers for paint where you can drop off your old half-used tins. Over 5,000 tonnes of waste paint is produced in Ireland annually according to the Rediscovery Centre in Dublin. Over 50 million litres of paint go to landfill and incineration every year in the UK. In 2020 Rediscover Paint sold 5,846 litres of recycled paint, saving 22 tonnes of CO_2. The Rediscovery Centre is engaged in a project to assess potential VOC emissions from their paint. You will need to

Paint containers left in recycling yard. (Photo: Rediscovery Centre)

Rediscover Paint. (Photo: Rediscovery Centre)

Mixing recycled paint. (Photo: Rediscovery Centre)

assure yourself that you are happy with recycled paints in terms of their emissions, chemical contents and quality as many are likely to be made from conventional, not eco paints. However, they may be cheaper than normal paints. Community Repaint in the UK, for instance, says they are sponsored by Dulux, so not all paint recycling is independent of the main paint companies.

Buyer Beware

Do not assume that because a paint is sold as 'eco' or '100 per cent VOC-free' that it is what it says it is. There are a few UK companies claiming to produce eco paints, but you are advised to be very cautious and check them out. One company in the north of England seems to change its registered address and its company registration number rather too frequently and they claim that their paints are 'eco certified' as ISO 14001. This is not a standard for certifying paints and is certainly not an eco classification; it is a standard for environmental management plans that can be used by any business. The Advertising Standards Authority have investigated this claim. The same company says that their paints are independently tested as having 0 per cent VOCs but they do not provide any information as to who carries out these tests; it is possible that the company directors also own a testing company. They say their health and safety data sheets are available on request but did not respond to a request! The terms 'natural', 'organic', 'eco' and 'vegan paints' are not protected in law so anyone can make such claims without having to justify them. The EU Paints Directive is in need of an update and regulation in the UK is inadequate.

Interior of house in Suffolk that has used a range of Biofa paints. (Photo: GreenSteps Ltd)

References

1. Tom Woolley, *Low Impact Building: Housing Using Renewable Materials* (Wiley, 2013).
2. EU Paint Directive 2004/42/EC.
3. https://www.diydoctor.org.uk/projects/eco-paints.htm
4. Roger Bilott, *Exposure: Poisoned Water, Corporate Greed, and One Lawyer's Twenty-Year Battle Against DuPont* (Simon & Schuster, 2019).
5. *Dark Waters*, 2019, starring Mark Ruffalo, director Todd Haynes.
6. 'Building a Better World: Eliminating Unnecessary PFAS in Building Materials', Green Science Policy Institute, at https://greensciencepolicy.org/our-work/building-materials/pfas-in-building-materials/
7. https://echa.europa.eu/documents/10162/23964241/09_ccb-durkin_en.pdf/a8ad3bdf-939c-46ae-7fcf-5657a0d15036
8. https://echa.europa.eu/documents/10162/23964241/01_cepe_van_der_meulen_en.pdf/076cf6fd-8065-364f-6f21-7ebe876295b1
9. https://www.biofapaint.co.uk/
10. https://www.auropaint.co.uk/
11. https://www.livos.de/en/
12. https://www.greensteps.co.uk/
13. https://www.livos.de/en/technical-data -sheets
14. https://osmouk.com/
15. https://osmouk.com/about/environment
16. https://earthbornpaints.co.uk/product/claypaint/
17. https://volvox.de/
18. http://ec.europa.eu/ecat/products/en/24236/ecotec-naturfarben-gmbh
19. https://www.healthyhomestore.co.uk/content/Earthborn/claypaint-msds.pdf
20. https://earthbornpaints.co.uk/faq/are-earthborn-paints-natural-and-organic/
21. https://www.motherearthnews.com/diy/casein-paint-zmaz06onzraw
22. https://homebuilding.thefuntimesguide.com/green_ways_how_to_remove_paint/
23. https://www.keimpaintshop.co.uk/
24. https://www.womersleys.co.uk/blog?Blog=142
25. https://www.beeck.com/en/products/bmf-product-category.php?k=mineral-paints
26. https://www.lehner-wool.com/en/silentum/
27. https://amorimcorkcomposites.com/en/materials-applications/consumer-goods/decoration/

Chapter Nine

RETROFIT AND RENOVATION

While many have dreams of building a new natural eco house, this is not readily available to those of us with limited budgets. Finding a site and an architect and builder who can deliver a house following the principles in this book is not easy and not everyone is able to become a self-builder. There are those brave souls who are willing to find a plot in rural west Wales and follow the One Planet Living system to create an off-grid, self-sufficient smallholding and house but this can be quite challenging. There are a few ecological land co-operative possibilities as well as co-housing and community land trust projects but these are few and far between. Finding an affordable site to buy and getting planning permission can be a bit daunting and less and less likely for young people.

The other option is to consider renovating the house that you already occupy, using natural materials to make it as healthy and natural as you can. Finding an old run-down building might be another option where you can get a lease or even buy it.

DIY improvement of existing homes is booming but you may have difficulty sourcing natural eco material from your local DIY store. However, many of the materials described in this book are also suitable for renovation and retrofit.

Permissions

It is important to remember that even apparently minor changes such as adding insulation, installing a new bathroom, changing your heating boiler and plumbing or adding an extension can all require building regulations approval and may require planning permission. Minor changes can fall under what is known as permitted development in planning law,

but you need to check this out. Work carried out that doesn't have approval may surface when you come to sell the house and so you then have to get retrospective permission. There are also many unscrupulous companies that will install insulation and carry out other work without getting building control approval and this can land you in trouble later on.

Getting Professional Advice

It may be difficult to find an architect who is interested in doing drawings and making applications for relatively minor works, but there are some who will. It is even harder to find one who understands natural and eco design principles.

There are many unqualified plandrawers or people who call themselves architects but aren't. You can check with the Architects Registration Board whether someone is a proper registered architect. (1) Sadly, the RIBA is a less reliable source as they have members who are not necessarily registered and there are many websites that list local architects but they also may not be registered. There are growing networks of young architects, such as the Architects Climate Action Network, (2) and many of them would be committed to using natural materials, but *warning* ... not all. In Scotland, there is the Scottish Ecological Design Association which has members who are interested in natural building. (3) Do beware of builders and installers who will claim to provide drawings and deal with building control. Some may do this competently but it is always best to check out previous projects they have done.

There are a range of community energy agencies around the UK and a few in Ireland. They are mostly engaged with promoting energy efficiency schemes but may be able to give you unbiased advice. (4) If you want advice on insulation or renewable energy and boiler replacement schemes then it is worth getting in touch. However, again be warned; many of them are not aware of or interested in the use of natural and healthy materials and may signpost you to private contractors who want to use toxic plastic flammable materials. There are very few grant schemes available but they may be able to advise on this.

Despite much talk of decarbonization and energy efficiency the British government have done little to incentivize insulating of homes and other efficiency measures. A recent English government 'Green Homes Grant' scheme has been an abject failure. (5)

Regional governments in Scotland and Wales have been a little better but Northern Ireland schemes are so limited that hardly anyone benefits. There are funding schemes in the Irish Republic but these are designed to promote the use of petrochemical and not natural materials. More detail on the terrible failures of insulation retrofit programmes are detailed later in this chapter and should be read to make sure that you don't fall victim to one of the many inadequate insulation retrofit programmes, some of which are even supported by local authorities.

Carbon Co-op and Other Organizations

On a more positive note there are some resident-run organizations that promote the use of environmentally friendly materials and give advice and run courses. One example is the Carbon Co-op in Manchester with their slogan 'People Powered not Fossil Fuelled'. (6) The Carbon Co-op has been assisting its members to retrofit their houses with mainly wood fibre insulation but have also run courses on hempcrete. They are currently establishing a new People Powered Retrofit agency. Many of the community energy projects around the country have tended to focus more on fitting solar photovoltaic (PV) panels to buildings or establishing solar farms and have not done enough to promote energy-saving measures. There is still a massive education programme required to ensure that even the green energy stalwarts understand the need to retrofit buildings with natural low embodied-energy materials. Community Energy Plus in Cornwall, for instance, where there are high levels of fuel poverty, only promote the installing of synthetic insulations. (7) A retrofit information hub in Herefordshire provides some useful contacts but some areas of the UK have nothing like this. (8)

Housing Co-operative members in Longsight, Manchester, hand-placing hempcrete onto a wall at a Carbon Co-op workshop with Graham Durrant and Tom Woolley. (Photo: Mat Fawcett)

However, don't let this lack of help put you off as there is much that can be done to an existing home that doesn't require a huge level of expertise or approvals and can make a big difference to your life.

Remedial Measures

Draughtproofing

Draughtproofing is a worthwhile affordable way to improve the energy efficiency of your house. The Energy Saving Trust appears to provide a useful guide but sadly provides no help with greener and healthier measures. Indeed, it contains really bad advice such as filling cracks in walls with cement or 'hard-setting fillers'. They also advocate the use of fillers, mastic and caulks, many of which contain toxic chemicals. (9) (10)

You can buy a range of draught excluders for doors and windows and while some are made from plastic, there are many made from aluminium, brushes and rubber and they can help to reduce draughts. Heavy curtains and fabric doorstoppers are also very useful.

Window Replacement

Replacing windows is expensive but may make a big difference to the thermal performance of your house. There are hundreds of door-to-door salespeople who will sell you uPVC replacement windows but if you can afford it try to use timber windows. It is possible to repair timber windows and fit secondary glazing. A tool company in Bury St Edmunds, Suffolk, provides a very well-illustrated guide on how you can repair timber windows. (11) If you search around you may be able to find a local company that has an environmental approach to making windows, such as George Barnsdale in Lincolnshire. (12)

If your house already has uPVC windows you may find that they are failing, as despite all the hype about PVC being maintenance-free, some don't last very long. However, you may not want to contribute even more PVC rubbish to landfill (as, despite claims of the PVC industry, very few are recycled). You may be able to find a local company that repairs them and make them more airtight so you can learn to live with them!

Good timber roof-lights are a worthwhile investment. While they are not cheap and there is work to do to the roof, etc., they can let a lot of beneficial light into the house while being quite energy-efficient. They also have an excellent trickle vent system that can help with draught-free natural ventilation as the warm stale air rises and escapes more easily through roof-lights. Velux provide an excellent guide to natural ventilation. (13)

Ventilation

Trickle vents are required in windows under the building regulations but they are often blocked up by occupants who think they are a source of draughts. Having inadequate ventilation can quickly lead to condensation and mould growth which are very bad for your health. Mould growth is frequently blamed on the lifestyle of occupants, whose behaviour involves anti-social activities like having baths and showers, washing and drying clothes and boiling things in the kitchen without remembering to turn on the extractor fan! Tenants of housing associations and private landlords are told to minimize how much moisture they produce when the main cause of the problem is inadequate ventilation and the use of synthetic materials like gypsum plasters and plastic paints. A natural eco house made from hygroscopic materials will deal much better with moisture, humidity and damp but it is still important to install good ventilation.

First of all, natural ventilation is best, so make sure there are trickle vents, but also open windows every morning: this is called purge ventilation. The British are apparently the worst at opening their windows whereas in some European countries 85 per cent of people throw their windows open every morning. Of course, if you live next to a heavily polluted traffic route, this may not be a good option.

Most houses have extractor fans in the bathroom and the kitchen but these may not be enough. Kitchen extractor filters should be changed regularly so choose one where it is easy to do this. Ordinary cheap extractor fans that come on when the light is switched on are next to useless and it is worth investing in a better product that has a humidistat. This will trickle away until there are high levels of moisture and then the fan will be boosted, which is a bit noisy but only for as long as necessary. Products made by Envirovent, Xpelair, Vent-Axia, Airflow and many others are worth the investment.

Mechanical ventilation and heat recovery is being promoted as a green zero-carbon solution but you do not need to go this far as they are expensive, some are noisy and require a great deal of maintenance, and you need to install ducts to all rooms and so on.

Dealing with Mould

If you have problems with mould, and a large number of UK houses suffer very badly, then you must first attend to the ventilation issue, but you can also use hygroscopic materials as finishes and for insulation that will regulate humidity. Some of the natural insulation materials and finishes described in this book will create a much healthier indoor environment. If your walls are covered in gypsum plaster and acrylic paints, this cannot deal with moisture as effectively and is more vulnerable to mould.

Try to avoid washing walls and windows down with bleach, which is often recommended for mould. Hydrogen peroxide is a useful greener alternative or baking soda and vinegar (distilled white vinegar) can be used.

Major Insulation Measures

Insulation materials are well covered in other chapters of the book; however, these can be used in renovation as well as newbuild.

An effective measure is to increase the insulation in the loft but make sure that you do not block up any vents at the sides of the roof. It is likely that your loft already includes old glass fibre insulation. Old insulation will have lost its 'loft' over time and not be as effective as it should be. Many people are allergic to the fibres and if you disturb the insulation in the roof you will find the fibres get into the house. The hatch to the roof should be well sealed to prevent this happening. You are faced with a choice of whether to get rid of the old dirty glass fibre insulation and replace it with something better. If you want to get rid of it then you will need to find a specialist extraction company. It should not be too hard to find a local extraction company as many insulation installers are making more money extracting old insulation (including mineral wool, foam, polystyrene and so on). You need to ensure that they have powerful extraction machines and that no dust and fibres contaminate the rest of the house or your neighbours. You should also ask where they are going to safely dispose of it!

Insulation Quilts

There are a range of insulation quilts outlined in this book that can be used in the loft, including sheep's wool, hemp, wood fibre, etc. However, if the loft has been converted or floored then you may have insulation between the rafters underneath the slates or tiles and this is a little trickier: you should get professional advice about this. There are dangers in ramming insulation everywhere in that it can cause problems with interstitial condensation dampness which may rot any wood in the roof or walls. Please do not fall prey to the spray foam insulation companies who will tell you that their product is healthy and breathable.

Spray foam is made from chemicals such as isocyanates. Some companies producing spray foam in the US have gone out of business due to the huge volume of class action lawsuits from people who say they became sick as a result of spray foam installation.

External wall insulation (EWI) can be done with wood fibre insulation or hempcrete but most companies and officially backed schemes use synthetic materials. Some of these, like mineral wool, are breathable depending on what other materials are used but some local authority schemes involve quite complex build-ups using non-breathable boards with brick facing. Plastic foam EWI materials should be avoided at all costs if you are concerned about fire safety, your health and the welfare of the planet. There are question marks over how effective they are as insulants too.

Cavity wall insulation (CWI) may seem like an attractive option and if you are lucky, and your walls are in good condition, it might be OK. Normally, polystyrene balls are injected into the walls. The installers don't really know what is going on in the cavity (even when they use cameras) nor do they know whether they have effectively filled it. Some people have had to campaign to get the polystyrene removed due to severe dampness problems. Some companies install glass fibre into cavities, or spray foam. Severe dampness can result from spray foam being injected and to remove it you have to demolish either the inner or outer wall of the house to remove the foam with angle grinders.

When renovating a house, many people opt for internal wall insulation (IWI). This usually involves installing plasterboard sheets that have been bonded to plastic foam insulation boards directly onto existing walls, or onto battens or plaster dabs. The plasterboard is glued (using toxic glues) to foam insulation materials such as the PIR (polyisocyanurate) that burned on Grenfell Tower. There are some sophisticated companies advocating this with laser-designed pre-made panels, though these are based on the use of petrochemical insulation materials.

Dry Lining with Natural Materials

Wood fibre boards and hempcrete can be used very effectively internally if you want to use internal insulation. Wood fibre boards can be placed directly onto existing walls. Often a plaster-like glue is used to adhere the boards to the existing walls, but the boards can also be attached by special screw fixings. In theory, there should not be a problem with dampness behind the boards as wood fibre is vapour-permeable, but it is important to ensure that any plaster and paint layer on top of the wood fibre boards is also breathable.

It is possible to do what is called a condensation risk analysis but most importantly you should ensure that the existing walls are not very damp and that the render or pointing externally is in good condition.

Pavadry wood fibre dry lining at a window. (Photo: Carbon Co-op)

Wood fibre board with adhesive ready to be applied directly to existing wall for internal insulation. (Photo: Carbon Co-op)

Wood fibre boards applied directly to wall. (Photo: Carbon Co-op)

vapour-permeable but also can cope with some dampness in the walls. The hempcrete can be sprayed onto existing walls or cast with temporary shuttering. It is also possible to use hempcrete blocks, particularly where it would be a problem making a bit of a mess with wet materials.

Cork and lime can be sprayed onto walls and this mixture is claimed to have a similar performance to hempcrete, though it is very expensive if used in a thick layer.

Sheep's wool is also sometimes used as an internal insulating material. It is important in this case not to

Hempcrete renovation to house in South Wales, showing battens and temporary shuttering boards. (Photo: Grant Avon)

Hempcrete can be applied directly to masonry walls both internally and externally. Providing the walls are clean and free of dust the hempcrete should adhere quite easily. Hempcrete is eminently

Hempcrete using plastic shuttering system; Manchester Carbon Co-op workshop.

Hempcrete applied to internal wall of house. (Photo: Grant Avon)

Same hempcrete wall completed, with shuttering removed immediately after casting.

Hempcrete applied to an external brick wall at a workshop organized by the Carbon Co-op.

Timber stud dry lining with sheep wool insulation.
(Photo: Philip Gregory)

Woodwool boards on walls and ceiling in same farmhouse.
(Photo: Philip Gregory)

place the wool directly onto the existing walls and to ensure there is a ventilated cavity. A timber frame is required into which the sheep's wool is placed and the interior face is then lined with plasterboard or preferably a more breathable material such as woodwool.

External wall insulation is normally carried out using insulation material such as polystyrene with a polymer render though there are some complicated systems using less flammable mineral wool insulations. Hempcrete can be sprayed or cast internally onto brick and masonry walls, as shown here. It can also be used on external wall surfaces providing there is not a problem with changing the outside appearance and that some measures can be taken to extend the roof overhang.

Lime plaster applied to woodwool boards in same farmhouse.
(Photo: Philip Gregory)

Who Can You Trust to Insulate Your House?

The UK government has established the TrustMark scheme to give the impression that insulation installers have some level of competence and government endorsement (14) but critics claim that TrustMark is too closely related to the installer companies and to the Cavity Insulation Guarantee Agency (CIGA). (15)

Groups campaigning for people known as the victims of botched insulation schemes have called for more independent scrutiny of the insulation industry after many installer companies went bankrupt following the collapse of various government schemes such as ECO. These grant schemes seem to come and go rather rapidly and the latest Green Homes Grant lasted less than a year. (16)

The British Standards Institute has established certification schemes known as PAS 2030 and PAS 2035. The former has the aim of providing a robust 'uniformly applicable specification' that will assist installers to demonstrate that their installation of energy efficiency improvement measures has met specification and customer requirements. PAS 2035 adds to this with a more specific framework related to retrofit works. While these heavily bureaucratic hoops that builders and installers have to jump through may seem useful, these standards do not set out the correct materials that need to be used and installers are still allowed to install non-breathable petrochemical materials while complying with the red tape. Such has been the high levels of criticism of these standards that a significant review is now under way.

Stewart Clements, Director of the HHIC, comments: 'The proposals are yet another example of unnecessary burden,' he says. 'Up to five "professionals" may be required for every installation and loopholes could mean that they don't have to actually be qualified. Bureaucratic delays could leave vulnerable people without heating and hot water.'

He also believes that PAS 2035 does not offer any demonstrable benefit to the industry or consumers.

'In most instances, the presumed additional red tape would be a detriment to both,' he says, 'particularly those having boilers installed or replaced under government-backed retrofit schemes such as ECO, which aims to tackle fuel poverty in the UK.

'These new rules may increase costs, create confusion and not provide any additional, meaningful safeguards to consumers. It would also, almost certainly, increase installation time, leaving those most in need potentially without heat or hot water while they wait for the boxes to be ticked.' (16) (17)

Newbuild Improvements

Information in the rest of the book should guide you to the materials to use in newbuild solutions (such as an extension) or a retrofit one (such as a garage conversion). There are even specialist companies that provide hempcrete home offices and garden cabins.

For many people having a gleaming new kitchen is the first priority when improving a house. TV advertising during COVID lockdown has focussed on women too ashamed of their kitchen for it to be seen as background when they are facetiming their friends and neighbours! Most kitchen companies manufacture carcassing, doors and worktops from composite wood products like MDF and many of the doors and drawers are coated with vinyl and lacquered finishes. There are companies offering to build kitchens with natural solid wood, stone and marble worktops and natural wood doors but these tend to be much more expensive, although preferable to the use of composite materials. (18)

Formaldehyde emissions from kitchen units and furniture can be high though a well-known Swedish company claim that they are constantly working to eliminate or reduce formaldehyde emissions. (19)

There are companies that produce aluminium kitchen units and doors but these may have been sprayed with a hazardous paint. It is also important to be careful about the adhesives used for tiles and sealants, though there are non-toxic alternatives available that claim to be VOC-free. (20)

Indoor Air Quality Improvements: What to Take Out of Your House

If you want a more natural and healthier house you can try to identify the sources of chemicals and pollutants. This can be done by carrying out an air sampling test using an indoor air home test kit. (21) You don't need to be a scientist to do this as you can hire a small sampling pump into which you insert supplied air sampling tubes. You send back the tubes and within a couple of weeks you will get a report telling you about the chemicals that have been detected that are emitting VOCs and formaldehyde. The test report should also give an indication of mould levels. The report will suggest possible sources of the VOCs and formaldehyde but you will then need to do some detective work to identify where these are.

You need to remove all the old tins of paint and brush cleaners and bottles of toxic cleaning materials that might have accumulated through the years, before you do the air sampling test. The indoor air pollution may also have come from outside traffic or industrial or agricultural pollution. There are various possible mitigation measures, including ventilation improvements, to reduce the impact of toxic chemicals in your house but you may need someone with expertise in this area to help deal with them. Hygroscopic absorbent materials such as sheep's wool and hempcrete insulation may help if there is an opportunity to install these. IKEA were advertising 'air-purifying' curtains (a product called Gunrid) which are still on their website, claiming to reduce air pollutants in the home, but it was impossible to obtain these as they had been withdrawn from sale and IKEA customer service never got back about this!

Air Purifiers

There are a wide range of electrical air-purifying electrical devices which contain filters costing in the region of £300 to £500. These normally only claim to deal with dust, pollen and allergens (bacteria and viruses maybe). However, it is unlikely that any will do anything about VOCs and formaldehyde though some claim to do so. It is essential to change the filters frequently or the unit will simply be spreading contaminated air back into the room. Most will only deal with a space the size of one room.

Paints and Finishes

When redecorating, pay close attention to the information contained in Chapter 8, which deals with paints.

What You Can Do as a Tenant

An increasing number of people are renting houses as they cannot afford to get on the property ladder. As a tenant, there is little you can do about the materials and finishes in the house or flat and unless you have a very unusual landlord they will not be interested in spending any money on improvements. Social housing landlords should be better than private landlords but this is not always the case.

There is no harm in carrying out an indoor air sampling test and complaining to your local Environmental Health Department if there are problems but it is unlikely that your environmental health officer, if they bother to visit, will have any expert knowledge about buildings. Local authority cuts and changing in training have had bad effects. Legislation to protect tenants in the UK is woefully inadequate and there are few sources of good advice. (22)

It can be quite easy for landlords to blame tenants for causing mould and damp; indeed local authorities and housing associations have been doing this for decades! The landlord might call in a damp 'expert' but they may not really be an expert and give entirely wrong advice. However, don't give up and put pressure on for something to be done.

There are a number of campaign groups who try to assist people who have been victims of botched retrofit schemes such as CIVALLI (Cavity Insulation Victims' Alliance) (23) and Fuel Poverty Action. (24) These, and other similar organizations, are run by unpaid volunteers and so they are unlikely to be able to help with technical solutions but they have drawn attention to the problem of retrofit disasters.

The Importance of Retrofitting Buildings and the Scandal of the Retrofit Disaster

Between 65 and 80 per cent of the existing building stock could still be standing in 2050 and so there is much to be done to improve and insulate these properties. An analysis of the problem can be found in Chapter 11 of a guide to insulation materials published by the Institute of Civil Engineers. (25) This chapter explains that 5.5 million houses in Britain do not have cavity wall insulation and 92 per cent of solid-walled houses have no insulation. This creates a problem known as fuel poverty for a significant proportion of the population who cannot afford to heat their poorly insulated houses. The Government Chief Construction Advisor in 2015 reported that: 'There were many instances of an incorrect solution having been applied in insulating solid-walled buildings, which in some cases has caused damp, mould or poor air quality. Little wonder then, the reluctance of homeowners to spend money retrofitting their properties if the outcome cannot be assured.' (25) The best-known disaster is in Preston but there have been many more throughout Scotland, England and Wales. (26) (27) (28)

Colin King of BRE Wales reported in 2016 that nearly 10 per cent of insulation works did not meet the necessary standards. The organization that was meant to guarantee cavity wall insulation, CIGA, had an unsatisfactory record of dealing with complaints, according to their own consumer champion, Teresa Perchard. (29)

A major study of cavity problems was commissioned in 2017/18 by the Northern Ireland Housing Executive (NIHE), employing BBA CIT to survey houses in Northern Ireland where cavity wall insulation had been carried out. The report revealed 63 per cent of installations were defective. (30)

While this is very depressing, the message is to take charge of your insulation retrofit as far as possible and to use the right materials. A further account of these issues can be found in a presentation given to the Sustainable Traditional Buildings Alliance (STBA) and the Society for the Protection of Ancient Buildings (SPAB). (31) A useful guide to sustainable retrofit has been published by the Scottish Ecological Design Association (SEDA). (32)

References

1. https://arb.org.uk/
2. https://www.architectscan.org/
3. https://www.seda.uk.net/
4. https://communityenergyengland.org/
5. https://www.current-news.co.uk/news/eac-slams-government-for-simply-abandoning-green-homes-grant
6. https://carbon.coop/
7. https://www.cep.org.uk/autumn-insulation-scheme-launch/
8. https://hgnetwork.org/wp-content/uploads/2021/02/Retrofit-Information-.pdf

9. https://energysavingtrust.org.uk/advice/draught-proofing/?gclid=EAIaIQobChMIh6Pot7uA8gIVye7tCh1F0gUBEAAYAiAAEgK_VfD_BwE

10. https://energysavingtrust.org.uk/cutting-out-draughts-older-homes/

11. https://www.festool.co.uk/knowledge/application-examples/refurbishing-wooden-windows#Procedure

12. https://www.georgebarnsdale.co.uk/blog/eco-friendly-windows/

13. https://www.velux.com/what-we-do/research-and-knowledge/deic-basic-book/ventilation/natural-ventilation-with-roof-windows?consent=preferences,statistics,marketing&ref-original=https%3A%2F%2Fwww.google.com%2F)

14. https://www.trustmark.org.uk/firms/Installers-UK-Ltd-1736241

15. https://ciga.co.uk/trustmark/

16. https://www.phamnews.co.uk/energy-efficiency-retrofits-to-face-increased-bureaucracy/

17. https://www.landlordtoday.co.uk/breaking-news/2020/12/warning-over-cowboy-builders-exploiting-green-homes-grant

18. https://woodandwoodkitchens.co.uk/low-voc-formaldehyde/

19. https://www.ikea.com/us/en/files/pdf/e1/12/e11228df/ikea_faq_formaldehyde.pdf

20. https://www.ecomerchant.co.uk/marmox-multibond-adhesive-sealant-300ml.html

21. https://www.waverton-iaq.com/

22. https://england.shelter.org.uk/housing_advice/repairs/damp_and_mould_in_rented_homes

23. http://www.civalli.com/home

24. https://www.fuelpovertyaction.org.uk/

25. Eshrar Latif, Rachel Bevan and Tom Woolley, *Thermal Insulation Materials for Building Applications* (ICE Publishing, 2019).

26. https://www.theconstructionindex.co.uk/news/view/hansford-recommends-solid-wall-insulation-drive

27. https://passivehouseplus.ie/news/health/disastrous-preston-retrofit-scheme-remains-unresolved

28. Sian Elin Dafydd, 18 April 2017, 'Cavity Wall Insulation a "Scandal", Arfon MP Claims', at https://www.bbc.com/news/uk-wales-politics-39602540

29. In 2019 BBC Radio 4 reported the issues many people are suffering from caused by cavity wall insulation. The report illustrates what can go wrong when cavity wall insulation is installed incorrectly. Refer to https://slscavityclaims.co.uk/ and https://stratuslegalsolutions.co.uk/radio-cavity-claims/

30. https://www.nihe.gov.uk/Working-With-Us/Research/Cavity-Wall-Insulation-Research-Project-2019

31. https://www.usablebuildings.co.uk/UsableBuildings/Unprotected/Breathable.pdf

32. https://www.seda.uk.net/products/sustainable-renovation-guide

Chapter Ten

CHALLENGES FOR THE FUTURE

This chapter includes a discussion of some of the problems about the failure of governments and even green campaigners to recognize the value of natural low embodied-energy materials and some advice about the hurdles you may have to surmount with your natural building project.

When Will the Love Affair with Flammable Toxic Plastic Insulation Materials End?

At 1am on 14 July 2017, residents in Grenfell Tower in West London woke to find their 24-storey tower block was on fire. Seventy-two people perished in the fire and the lives of hundreds more who escaped, or lived nearby, have been permanently scarred. What, you might ask, does this have to do with natural building? Grenfell was a disaster waiting to happen and symbolizes the failure of petrochemical-based insulation materials. Natural non-flammable materials could be used to make buildings safer. As has subsequently been realized, hundreds of tower blocks have been covered with dangerous cladding and insulation and many more lives have been wrecked by the sluggish response to this problem, affecting social housing tenants and also homeowners who have put their life savings into an apartment, many of whom are now facing bankruptcy. Grenfell reflects a construction industry that had fallen hook, line and sinker for the idea that buildings could be upgraded with 'cheap' flammable petrochemical-based materials. As has emerged in the Grenfell Inquiry, the system of testing, checking and approving these insulation materials and cladding systems was fundamentally flawed and companies have been alleged to have lied and cheated in the pursuit of profit. This book is not the place to document this in detail, but much of what will be written by others is unlikely to ask about what alternative materials could have been used, as there remains an assumption that synthetic insulation materials are the only things available. This is despite the damage this does to the environment during production and the subsequent damage to the health of occupants.

When visiting Grenfell just a few weeks after the disaster it was clear that the authorities had not even bothered to clear up after the fire. Residents were able to pick up lumps of toxic fire residue that were lying around housing, gardens and even children's playgrounds. This can be seen in a video interview recorded by Grenfell Speaks (1) when the problem of toxic residue in the North Kensington area was first raised.

Grenfell Tower after the fire.

Public Health England and other bodies denied that there were increased risks to health around Grenfell as the levels of toxicity were the same as generally found in London, which was hardly reassuring. (2) The government commissioned global consulting firm AECOM to study the risk to residents from contamination in the area but they found nothing worrying! (AECOM are in a joint venture with Capita to carry out Phase 2b of the HS2 high speed rail project.) The government also refused to carry out blood tests on the survivors to see whether they had been subject to contamination from the chemicals released during the fire. (3)

There is a shocking head-in-the-sand attitude towards the use of toxic materials in buildings. A new law has been introduced to improve safety in buildings over 18 metres but will sadly be inadequate to address the real changes that are needed. There were 156,000 fires in the UK in 2020 attended by fire brigades, many of which were in houses *under* 18 metres in height. The number of fires is increasing year on year and they become more and more dangerous, especially for firefighters, who are exposed to the toxic chemicals released in fires. There has been substantial research carried out into smoke toxicity but no regulations in the UK or Europe to restrict the use of materials which emit toxic smoke. Firefighters are twice as likely to die of cancer, for instance. (4) Despite these concerns, plastic foam insulations continue to be sold in large quantities. The growing use of lightweight construction with highly flammable foam insulation materials makes the situation much worse. Housing developers have been called to account for their failure to install proper fire stopping in recent developments, leading to massive levels of remedial works. (5) However, if houses were built with natural safer materials, then the current problems could be reduced.

Solar Panel Fires

Another worrying source of fires is from solar panels, which many people are fitting to their roofs in the hope

PUR and PIR boards like these are widely available in builders' merchants.

that this will reduce their electricity costs. Some innovative, publicly funded, low-energy projects are even fitting solar panels to walls, backed with exactly the same insulation that burned on Grenfell Tower. Many people are tempted by rent-a-roof schemes where they allow a private company to install panels on their roofs and put a charge on their property, which can lead to all sorts of problems in the future with mortgages and insurance. With flammable synthetic insulations in roofs, this can lead to greater property damage when faulty solar panels burst into flames. So serious is the problem that the Building Research Establishment Solar Centre produced a report about this. (6) The manufacture of solar panels, mostly in China, is also alleged to lead to serious pollution (7) and while green campaigners call for solar panels on every house, little thought is given to the environmental impact and risks associated with this.

Howard Liddell warned of these dangers in a brilliant little book in 2008, in which he coined the term 'ecobling'. (8) There are great dangers from the emphasis

Solar panel following fire.

Damage inside a house following fire in roof caused by defective solar panel.

put on technological solutions to the climate crisis that are frequently advocated by green campaign groups, which have been described by American writer Kristine Mattis as 'techno-salvation'. (9) Many people who want to build or improve their homes assume that the first step is to use expensive technological equipment such as heat pumps, mechanical ventilation and solar panels, while overlooking the need to insulate the house first. An important element of this book is to encourage people away from techno-salvation to do simple and natural things such as using natural materials. In an ideal world, we should all be able to benefit from solar power; however, in the UK warm water solar systems were virtually killed off by government regulation and takeovers by the petrochemical insulation industry. Many PV panels have been installed by cowboy companies, even with the support of local authority energy schemes, and even though the installers have long gone, shadow companies that continue to collect the income from them continue. For many people, it is not feasible, due to lack of space, but solar panels are best located in a position away from your roof on a separate structure if you are attempting to live off-grid.

The Myth of Decarbonization

It is easy for governments and local authorities to pass resolutions about achieving zero carbon by a certain date, without actually doing much about it, and there are literally hundreds of reports published by a wide range of bodies such as the UK Green Building Council, the Construction Leadership Council and many green campaign groups calling for decarbonization, without ever spelling out how this will be achieved in practice. One thing you can be certain of is that none of these reports say anything much about how to insulate buildings to make them more energy-efficient. Having reviewed over fifty such recent reports, it can be confirmed that the word 'insulation' is barely mentioned. These reports do not mention the use of low embodied-energy materials and products and there will be nothing in there about natural insulations. Some organizations do talk about embodied energy but fail to spell out what this means in terms of specifying building materials and solutions. There are plenty of computer-based tools now available to architects to calculate embodied energy but this does not necessarily lead to a reduction in the use of petrochemical and concrete materials. One of the more progressive groups, ACAN (Architects Climate Action Network), issued a fifty-six-page report in February 2021 about embodied carbon which only mentions insulation five times. This report is better than most: it does briefly mention bio-based materials (Policy Z2) but provides barely any explanation. It states the need for 'introducing a requirement for the use of low carbon and ecologically beneficial materials' but only in 'designated development areas', whatever that means. Anyone reading the ACAN report would assume that they are only talking about the increased use of timber, as they give little guidance on the nature and use of low embodied-energy materials. (10)

This is a massive problem for the natural materials industry because without policy documents spelling out the importance of a rapid change away from high embodied-energy materials to bio-based, natural and recycled materials, the industry will just continue with business as usual. When debating with the natural materials deniers they will quickly argue that it would be impossible to scale up production of natural materials and so it's necessary to continue with what is often referred to as 'shovel-ready technology'. This is a classic catch-22 situation, which plays into the hands of the big businesses importing chemical materials from China. Unless there is greater demand for low embodied-energy materials, it may not be economically feasible to scale up production. Natural building deniers will tell you straightaway that hemp is no solution as we cannot reduce food production to use land to grow hemp (forgetting that hemp itself is also a food crop). Some are opposed to the use of hemp due to the fact that hemp comes from the same plant family as cannabis and marijuana. Industrial hemp varieties contain negligible THC (tetrahydrocannabinol), the drug content, but farmers could earn a good living from growing hemp if they were allowed to harvest the flowers for the medicinal CBD (cannabidiol). Other natural building detractors will quickly refer to moths in sheep's wool and tell you that wood fibre insulation burns too easily. It would be useful to know who is circulating this negative propaganda about natural materials.

Super-Insulating: the Problem of Passivhaus

A big problem to overcome is the argument that it is essential to go to extreme lengths to make buildings super-energy-efficient and some say that this cannot be achieved with natural materials. Here there is a fundamental problem in that extreme energy efficiency costs a lot of money and is outside the pockets of most people but, in any case, is not as effective as is frequently claimed. This can be illustrated by discussing passivhaus. Passivhaus has had a malign influence on environmental approaches to building because its adherents justify the use of high embodied-energy materials and solutions on the basis that it will lead to zero energy consumption. This is a false and dangerous approach but has been readily accepted by official bodies wanting

Hemp plant legally growing on farm in Co. Kerry, Ireland.

to clutch onto some ready-made approach to saving energy, without really understanding its implications.

There are a few projects illustrated in this book where attempts have been made to achieve passivhaus standards using natural materials such as straw bales, but by and large passivhaus proponents prefer to use petrochemical-based materials with plastic airtightness membranes and synthetic tapes. Passivhaus originated in Germany, but leading sustainable building experts there soon offered an alternative called 'aktivhaus', with a clear attack on the principles of passivhaus. (11) Lee Marshall of UK consultants Viridis Building Services offers a reasoned critique of passivhaus in *Architecture Today* magazine, claiming that passivhaus rules will only produce a marginal energy saving, compared with a less costly approach for a standard $235m^2$ house (12). Marshall sets out the costs of this marginal energy saving and argues that the extra costs of passivhaus would be £21,500. He also is very critical of mechanical ventilation and heat recovery systems which are standard in passivhaus projects, claiming that they generally only recover a few degrees of heat, necessitating electric heaters to make up the shortfall. If you are tempted to sign up to passivhaus then it might be worth thinking again as it is not an independently verified standard but a private business initiative, making profits out of certification of buildings and products.

Organizations initially founded to promote ecological building, such as the Association for Environment Conscious Building (AECB), the Alliance for Sustainable Building Products (ASBP), the Green Register and many more, give mixed messages by being associated with passivhaus, while sometimes stating support for natural materials as well. Passivhaus is actively supported by the main petrochemical-based insulation manufacturers.

Getting Approvals, Insurance and Mortgages

People considering natural building and materials often worry about whether there will be problems in getting mortgages and insurance. For many, this can appear to be a barrier to using natural materials. A number of alternative insurance and mortgage providers were contacted in an effort to determine their policies on such materials. It wasn't possible to survey a wide range of organizations, but the Ecology Building Society were very helpful in providing the following statement:

Our lending decisions always involve considering the overall positive environmental or social impact of any given property or project. It is this case-by-case analysis that steers us away from defining a detailed list of specific building materials that will preclude a project from consideration on the basis of a single feature ... We'll always consider non-standard building materials and construction types such as timber-frame, straw bale, rammed earth and earth sheltered dwellings. As well as traditional construction and listed buildings, we also embrace modern methods of construction and innovative ways of building using technology such as structural insulated panels (SIPs), insulated concrete forms and other off-site approaches.

When reviewing case study examples of projects funded by the Ecology Building Society, it was striking how many used petrochemical and non-*ecological* materials but despite this they have also supported projects using natural materials. (13)

Other mainstream banks and mortgage lenders are difficult to pin down when it comes to policies on materials. There has been some nervousness about timber frame construction in the past, but providing projects have a certificate from an architect, building control and a home-building registration body there should not be a problem. One piece of advice is not to go into great detail about the materials that have been used as the bank or building society official will not have much, if any, building expertise or qualifications.

There is also nervousness about insurance for buildings with natural materials and an attempt was made to get a policy statement from the Association of British Insurers, which was a futile waste of time.

Structural insulated panels (SIPs) made with polystyrene.

An insurance broker in Totnes, Naturesave Insurance, was more helpful and they explain on their website that they provide ethical 'bespoke' insurance cover for homes that are unique: 'From a simple Eco-Home to an award-winning grand design, many of today's houses use cutting-edge construction techniques and technology. Conversely, many existing properties have been constructed using non-standard construction techniques like timber frame or wattle and daub.' (14)

Numerous projects constructed with hempcrete and strawbales have been insured by mainstream companies who recognize what they call 'non-standard' home insurance. This is a somewhat bizarre concept as insurance companies view standard construction as a typical 1930s brick cavity-wall semi-detached, a type which is rarely built today, and so most buildings today are non-standard. It is essential to be honest in any statement to insurance companies, as when a claim is made the assessor is always looking for ways to avoid paying the claim. Assessing insurance risk is not an exact science, and a brick-faced house full of flammable foam insulation may well be regarded as less of a risk than an unusual hempcrete house, even though the latter can be much more effective at resisting a fire.

When budgeting for your natural house project, it's worth factoring in that you may have to pay a little more for the mortgage or insurance.

Getting planning permission and building regulations approval can also be a barrier as you can still be dealing with people and officials who may put obstacles in your way. It is best to be prepared for such problems and prepare a good case by having details of other projects that are not too far away that have already been approved using cob, straw or hemp, etc. Generally speaking, planning restrictions will be about the external appearance and the planners should not dictate what materials you use for insulation. With building regulations, if you can provide sufficient technical evidence that the structural and thermal performance standards will be met there should not be a problem in theory, but some officials can still be hostile. In Wales, the One Planet development rules will be an additional hurdle and others try to use obscure legislation such as the Caravan Act to claim that their natural building can be moved or at least dismantled. Contacting someone who has gone through the process before is always enormously helpful as you can learn from their experience.

A good piece of advice is not to go bounding enthusiastically into the local authority office at an early stage to tell them that you are planning to build a natural house, though this often happens. Assuming that plans for a sustainable low-impact house will meet recent local authority statements about decarbonization can meet with disappointment since the planning policies were often written twenty years ago. Preparing to build or renovate or extend needs a carefully planned campaign with a strategy and tactics worked out with the advice of professionals. Many people with limited budgets are loath to spend money on architects and planning consultants and often forge ahead without such advice. This can be a mistake, sometimes costing more than the professional fees that they had hoped to save, in additional costs of planning appeals and so on. In an ideal world, it would be good not to be so dependent on specialists and professionals and there are cases where unqualified laypeople have produced their own home-made drawings and secured approvals. The Welsh One Planet policy was meant to support this.

Standards for Natural Materials

A further barrier to getting approval for projects can be the lack of certificates and standards for natural materials. There is nothing that bureaucrats like better than a trail of pieces of paper. Certification of products and systems costs tens of thousands of pounds or euros and this is beyond the reach of cob or hemp builders. Despite this, some approvals are available and can be used to support applications such as the LABSS certificate for hempcrete referred to in Chapter 6. Justification of the sustainability of proposals, as requested by official bodies, can involve reference to something like the BRE Green Guide to Specification (15) even though it can be argued that their assessments favour unsustainable petrochemical materials and rarely include natural bio-based or low-impact materials. (16) Getting an energy rating (EPC) or a thermal performance prediction (SAP) can be done fairly easily in the UK but is more difficult in Ireland where BER assessors have said that they cannot assess hempcrete and other bio-based buildings. On the other hand, these are hurdles that have to be overcome and just one of the many battles that have to be fought. (17)

While this book was in preparation there was an opportunity to submit evidence to the UK government about energy efficiency and future building standards and some submissions have been made about the importance of bio-based materials. (18) (19) However, we are a long way from the UK and regional governments embracing the value of natural materials and indeed they are still more likely to promote high-tech petrochemical-based approaches for the foreseeable future, as they still do not understand the importance of embodied energy and the other negative aspects of conventional construction.

Healthy Buildings

A further gap is the lack of standards for healthy buildings and good indoor air quality. Currently, anyone can sell 'healthy houses', even when they contain materials off-gassing unpleasant chemicals. There are a handful of architects who subscribe to the German Building Biology principles, but this has not been widely adopted in the UK. Some consultants offer the American 'Well' building standard but this is so expensive that it has only been applied to a handful of office and commercial developments. The UK National Institute for Health and Care Excellence (NICE) are consulting on domestic indoor air quality guidelines (20) but indoor air pollution is barely on the agenda of the people writing the building regulations. There is talk of tightening up the European Construction Product Regulations (CPR) to restrict product emissions. You will find a CE mark on a bag of cement but this tells you little more than it is a bag of cement rather than confirming its environmental or health impacts. If emissions are regulated more stringently throughout Europe, this will affect the UK as well, and should work in favour of natural bio-based materials as most have very low if not zero emissions. Smoke toxicity regulations will also help if they are introduced. The building materials industry is talking of EU Health Product Declarations (HPDs), which already exist to a limited extent in the US. However, the lead on this is being taken by materials companies that have the most to lose if such declarations were to have any teeth.

It is best to be suspicious of some claims that materials and products are healthy and eco. Greenwashing and wellwashing are widespread and hopefully this book will help you steer your way through this environmental jungle. It's essential for those who embrace the beauty of natural materials that they understand they are part of a battle to change the way we build for the future.

An Association of Natural Builders?

Natural building organizations are weak compared with the organizations that bang the energy-efficiency-first drum so effectively. When carrying out research for this book, conversations with many people have been encouraging in that there is talk of establishing a network or alliance of the many young

Participants at hempcrete workshop at Heritage Ltd in Northern Ireland, casting hempcrete against concrete block wall.

businesses providing training, advice and building services who wish to avoid oil-based materials. Currently, strawbale builders, cob and earth builders, hempcrete builders, lime builders and timber construction businesses tend to operate in silos and do not collaborate sufficiently, but this may change in the future as many projects can involve the use of all these materials and technologies. Advocating a holistic approach that considers embodied-energy, health and pollution impacts and the effectiveness of natural materials, while minimizing or excluding plastics, is likely to gain in strength in the future.

References

1. 'Grenfell Speaks with Tom Woolley', interview, at https://www.youtube.com/watch?v=utHyWZUosAg
2. https://www.gov.uk/government/news/environmental-checks-around-grenfell-tower-show-no-increased-risk-to-health
3. https://assets.publishing.service.gov.uk/government/uploads/system/uploads/attachment_data/file/837842/Stage_1_Overarching_Report.pdf
4. https://www.chroniclelive.co.uk/news/north-east-news/firefighters-cancer-risk-safety-bbc-17000646
5. https://www.ifsecglobal.com/fire-news/missing-fire-barriers-in-new-build-homes-raises-concerns-over-training/
6. *Fire and Solar PV Systems – Investigations and Evidence: BRE Report P 100874-1004*, BRE National Solar Centre, Issue 2.9, 11 May 2018.
7. https://www.forbes.com/sites/michaelshellenberger/2018/05/23/if-solar-panels-are-so-clean-why-do-they-produce-so-much-toxic-waste/#474c6841121c
8. Howard Liddell, *Eco-Minimalism: The Antidote to Eco-Bling* (RIBA Publishing, 2008).
9. https://www.counterpunch.org/2019/03/04/theres-nothing-radical-about-the-green-new-deal/
10. ACAN, 'The Carbon Footprint of Construction', February 2021, at https://www.architectscan.org/embodiedcarbon and https://765bf7ec-2dd0-4cf7-9b76-f2f379ab6a0f.filesusr.com/ugd/b22203_c17af553402146638e9bc877101630f3.pdf
11. Manfred Hegger, Caroline Fafflok, Johannes Hegger and Isabell Passig, *Aktivhaus – The Reference Work: From Passivhaus to Energy-Plus House* (Birkhauser, 2016).
12. Lee Marshall, 'Is Passivhaus Overrated?' *Architecture Today*, July–August 2021, 56–57.
13. https://www.ecology.co.uk/projects/
14. https://www.naturesave.co.uk/
15. https://www.bregroup.com/greenguide/podpage.jsp?id=2126
16. https://goodhomes.org.uk/wp-content/uploads/2017/05/GHA-Critique-of-the-Green-Guide-to-Specification-051208.pdf
17. https://selfbuild.ie/advice/building-with-hempcrete/4/
18. https://committees.parliament.uk/work/309/energy-efficiency-of-existing-homes/
19. https://www.gov.uk/government/consultations/the-future-buildings-standard
20. https://www.nice.org.uk/guidance/ng149